Children of Divorce

Children of Divorce

DEBBIE BARR

7891

ZondervanPublishingHouse
Grand Rapids, Michigan

A Division of HarperCollinsPublishers

Children of Divorce
Copyright © 1986, 1992 by Debbie Barr

Requests for information should be addressed to:
Zondervan Publishing House
Grand Rapids, Michigan 49530

Library of Congress Cataloging-in-Publication Data

Barr, Debbie.
   [Caught in the crossfire]
   Children of divorce / Debbie Barr.
      p. cm.
   Previously published as: Caught in the crossfire. c1986.
   Includes bibliographical references.
   ISBN 0-310-28741-3 (pbk.)
   1. Children of divorced parents. 2. Family—Religious life.
3. Children of divorced parents—United States. I. Title.
[HQ777.5.B375 1992]
646.7'8—dc20   92–10003
                                                      CIP

Formerly published as *Caught in the Crossfire*

Edited by James E. Ruark, Lisa Garvelink, and Evelyn Bence

Cover designed by Terry Dugan

Printed in the United States of America

99 00 / DH / 9 8 7

To Christopher Matthew Barr

CONTENTS

PART FIVE
Healing Propositions

MATT AND KIM
A Read-Aloud Story for Children

ACKNOWLEDGMENTS

This is a thank-you note to the many people who made special contributions to both the first and second editions of this book.

My sincere thanks goes first to my twenty-six-member "panel of experts"—the children of divorce and single parents who graciously and openly shared their personal experiences and thoughtful insights on the subject of divorce. Their lives and words have been woven into the heart of this book and into my own heart as well. Throughout the book their names have been changed, and on this page they remain anonymous, except to say that they are from nine different states—Tennessee, Nebraska, North Carolina, Florida, Pennsylvania, Georgia, Arkansas, Wisconsin, and Louisiana.

Several friends across the country helped locate these children and single parents for interviews. Others shared professional advice, loaned a computer, typed, or took time out of busy schedules to read the manuscript and offer suggestions. I am indebted to these people for their various contributions: Ruth Moore, Dr. Gary Chapman, Dr. Dan Meyer, Darrell Barr, Dave and Sue Imbrock, Maureen Stahle, Christine Gale, David Martin, Don Mann, Jan Hipp, Lynn Parsley, Jackie Mackie, John Schweighart, Sharon Fausch, Pam Harrelson, Sheryl Fink, Judy Couchman, Tim Wilkins, Liz and Joe May, Andrea Buczynski, Diane Serge, and Loraine Clewis.

I am indebted to several authors whose works especially stimulated my thinking and provided a wealth of information about children and divorce: Judith S. Wallerstein and Joan Berlin Kelly (*Surviving the Breakup*), Judith S. Wallerstein and Sandra Blakeslee (*Second Chances: Men, Women and Children a Decade After Divorce*), Linda Bird Francke (*Growing Up Divorced*), Archibald Hart (*Children and Divorce*), and Henry B. Biller (*Paternal Deprivation; Father, Child, and Sex Role; Father Power*).

Finally, and most of all, I want to thank the many friends who offered support, encouragement, and prayer all along the way, when the manuscript was originally written in 1984 and when it was updated in 1992.

Feel the dignity of a child. Do not feel superior to him, for you are not.
—Robert Henri

INTRODUCTION

Growing up in a small Pennsylvania town, I was not aware of divorce. As far as I knew then, no one in my family had ever been divorced, and I knew of only one child who had divorced parents. The topic of divorce rarely entered my thoughts or conversations. It was not part of the world in which I lived.

But times have changed. Today, I know a great many people who have experienced divorce. Friends, neighbors, and members of my extended family are divorced. People I have worked with through the years, and many people at my church are divorced. After I was grown and married, my own parents divorced each other. In stark contrast to my childhood perceptions, divorce now seems to be everywhere—and so are the children whose lives it touches.

Today two out of every five children are children of divorce.[1] One out of two marriages ends in divorce, and experts believe that this trend will continue. If analysts are correct, 40 percent of our nation's children will see their parents divorce before the children reach the age of eighteen.[2]

In 1950 divorce ended 385,144 American marriages. The number of children touched by those divorces is estimated at 299,000.[3] Now, more than forty years later, the rise in these figures is dramatic. In 1990 The National Center for Health Statistics recorded 1,175,000 divorces. With those decrees, more than one million children became children of divorce.

In fact, more than a million children have seen their parents divorce every year since 1972.[4] Half of all divorces involve children, and each year roughly 2 percent of our total child population joins the ranks of the children of divorce.[5] That means after two decades of epidemic divorce, the cumulative total of children affected tops twenty million.

The reasons for divorce are myriad, but over time some patterns have emerged. It is known, for example, that nearly 56 percent of separated or divorced people have been exposed to familial alcoholism, either growing up with an alcoholic, marrying one, or having a blood relative who is an alcoholic.[6] The economic hardships, physical and psychological abuses, and social isolation created by alcoholism render the family unit dysfunctional and in many ways predispose it to divorce. Even when alcohol is no longer present, its effects persist in unhealthy family practices and relational patterns.

Divorce often can be traced to other kinds of family dysfunction. A dysfunctional family may be characterized by emotional repression or a rigid, dogmatic environment. It may involve a family member's compulsive use of food, sex, gambling, or drugs. There may be emotional, verbal, sexual, or physical abuse. Workaholism, eating disorders, mental illness, and even handicaps can render a family dysfunctional and burden it with problems that can pave the way to divorce. Some members of dysfunctional families function well outside the realm of family, but within the family they do not interact in healthy ways.

It is also known that second marriages, especially those that include children from first marriages, are particularly prone to failure. This means that many children's lives are impacted not once, but twice (or more) by divorce.

Many people feel profound compassion for the children caught in the crossfire between divorcing parents. They care about these kids and would like to help them, but they're unsure about what to do. This book, which has grown out of my own compassion and concern for the children of divorce, is written for those special, caring people with a heart to help. It is my hope that many children whom they love, but whom I will never meet, will be enriched and encouraged as a result of this book.

PART ONE

WHEN THE BOUGH BREAKS

1
The Children of Divorce

I think divorce is now a normal part of life. It's hard for kids nowadays, but most kids can adjust. But some kids can't.
—Anna, age seventeen

Ryan is not quite three years old, but he knows how it feels when a mommy and a daddy get divorced: It's scary and it makes you cry. It's so hard to understand where Mommy is and why she doesn't come back home where she belongs. Divorce isn't much fun, but it sure helps to have an older brother and a daddy and a grandpa who stick close to you through it all.

Ten-year-old Paige knows a lot about divorce. Her family got a separation five years ago, and then they got a divorce a few years later. It really hurts when your mom and dad don't see eye to eye on the most important things in life, and it can cause some terrible problems, especially financial. It's hard, too, when your daddy doesn't call you for months on end and even forgets your birthday! It makes you wonder if he cares.

Sarah, fifteen, has some definite opinions about divorce in general and about her parents' divorce in particular. It's hard not to judge her father when it seems that what he's done is so obviously wrong. "It's really weird for me to hate and love somebody at the same time," she admits. Seeing her mom cry makes her cry, too. Sometimes she feels scared, sometimes bitter. Depression comes and goes.

Things in Terry's family were never really right. His parents separated when he was a baby and finally divorced when he was thirteen. Now in his late twenties, Terry would be the first to admit that he is still bothered by the way his parents' relationship affected his childhood. In fact, he still feels uneasy, as if something very important was never settled. Trying to figure out just what went wrong and how to avoid making the same mistakes is a major preoccupation. The hurt just never goes away, no matter how many years go by.

Ryan, Paige, Sarah, and Terry are part of one of our nation's fastest growing population groups. They are the children of divorce.

Our high rate of divorce may have been fueled by the popular perception that divorce is a problem solver and one not all that harmful to children. After all, it seems reasonable that if the adults aren't happy in the marriage, the children can't be happy either. If divorce is a solution for the adults, it makes sense to assume the kids will benefit, too. A second, equally comforting thought is that children are resilient. They bounce back quickly from divorce. Even if they don't like the idea at first, they will get used to it. And because they are young, they will probably adjust even better than their parents.

As reassuring as these ideas are, they are false. Before the late teen years, virtually no child will agree that his or her parents' should have divorced. Research indicates that few children (less than 10 percent) experience relief of any kind when their parents divorce. Rather, the experience is unpleasant and far from insignificant—an emotional earthquake, an unparalleled crisis that roars through their lives making sweeping changes without their consent.

Divorce researcher Judith Wallerstein* found that even five years after divorce 56 percent of the children interviewed felt

---

*In 1971 psychologist Judith S. Wallerstein began a comprehensive study of the effects of divorce on children and their families. Sixty families, including 131 children between the ages of two and eighteen, were involved in the research. Initially, each adult was interviewed six times and each child three or four times. They were interviewed one year later and again at the five-, ten-, and fifteen-year marks, enabling the researchers to trace the effects of divorce over time. This study, the California Children of Divorce Project, was the first to examine the long-range effects of divorce on children; because of this I refer to it frequently.

that divorce had made little or no improvement in their family life. Only about a third of the children she observed bounced back with the resiliency that most adults expect to see. The 101 children who were interviewed five years after their parents' divorces varied widely in their adjustment. From a psychological point of view, 34 percent "appeared to be doing especially well," 29 percent "were in the middle range of psychological health," and 37 percent were "consciously and intensely unhappy and dissatisfied with their life in the postdivorce family."[1]

Each divorce is unique, and each child affected by divorce is unique. Even children within a family do not all respond to parental divorce in the same way, as age, temperament, and other factors play a part in mediating individual response. In general terms, however, the more hostile the relationship between parents, and the more stresses and changes that simultaneously confront a child, the harder it is to bear up under divorce.

It now appears that many of the difficulties children experience after divorce stem not only from the divorce and its aftermath, but also from a history of family problems prior to divorce. Studies have shown a direct connection between "spousal conflict and poor behavior and emotional adaptation in children, within both intact and divorcing families."[2] Many children must cope not only with divorce, but also with the effects of having spent the formative years of their lives in the context of a dysfunctional family. This may provide a partial explanation of why some children do well and others do poorly in the years following the divorce.

THE IRONY

There's a great and sad irony in divorce: Just as a child's needs for security and reassurance escalate in the face of impending divorce, parental capacity for meeting those needs diminishes greatly.

Brandon, a divorced father of two, reflected on the time just before he and his wife separated: "The problem with that time is that your whole mind and all your efforts are pointed in the direction of trying to work things out or trying to figure out what's going on. So you tend to neglect your kids at that time. You're very short with them. You just don't give them the time that you normally do. They don't know what's going on. The only thing that could really be better—and I don't know if it's humanly possible—is to try to think of them more and try to spend more time with them and not be so short-tempered. I think that's probably the time they suffered the most.''

Understandably, parents in great emotional distress have trouble dealing with their children's pain. Even when they consciously recognize that a child is hurting, parents may not be able to muster enough emotional energy to lay aside their own concerns and reach out to the child. Some tend to downplay what a child is feeling to keep the child's pain from adding guilt to their already overwhelming hurt and anxiety.

Some parents are oblivious to what their children are experiencing. Preoccupied with their own problems, they may interpret quietness, withdrawal, or unusually good behavior as good adjustment or nonchalance. Though this is unlikely, parents often have a strong need to believe it—at least until they regain their own equilibrium.

Discovering later how a child actually experienced the divorce may be unsettling. When *Newsweek* reporter Linda Francke began to research the topic of divorce and children, she interviewed her own daughters. Although she knew that they had been unhappy about her divorce from their father three years before, she was aghast to discover the extent of their crisis. In her book *Growing Up Divorced,* she recalls her reaction after interviewing her younger daughter. ''I was struck dumb by my maternal ignorance. How could I have failed to pick up the distress signals that she must have been sending out? I could have comforted her, reassured her, at least *listened* to her. And why hadn't she told me all this before? 'Because you never asked,' she said with a grin.''

That night, Francke writes, ''I lay awake, wondering whether other divorced or separated parents knew what their children were thinking, feeling, fantasizing, scheming, suffering. For even though my children and I led very close and interdependent lives, I never had a clue any of this was going on.''[3]

Dr. Wallerstein found that depression often makes it difficult for divorcing parents to console their children: "Sometimes in attempting to comfort the child, the parent would reexperience his own anguish and sob along with the grieving offspring. Children might then become alarmed at the impact of their distress on their parents, and learn to refrain from expressing their sadness or seeking solace."[4]

More than half of the children in Wallerstein's study felt that their fathers were "entirely insensitive to their distress" and more than one-third felt this way about their mothers.[5] Younger children tended to be better cared for than older ones, and these older children "were acutely aware of the lapses in parenting and felt aggrieved and neglected."[6] Almost every nine- or ten-year-old boy felt completely neglected by his father, and many girls felt that their mothers had emotionally abandoned them.[7]

Divorce presents many children with an unprecedented problem. In other upsetting times such as a bad storm, an illness, or an argument with a playmate, the children have turned to the parents for consolation. Now the parents are the *source* of the trauma and are increasingly unavailable as comforters. Not only are the children facing the greatest crisis of their young lives, but they are doing so without the emotional support of their parents. Other significant adults—teachers, neighbors, relatives, Sunday school teachers—may be unaware of the children's plight, or, if aware, they may have no idea how to help them cope. Often children feel as if there is no adult at all to whom they can turn; consequently they hobble along emotionally, dealing as best they can with a situation that may make almost no sense to them.

All in all, divorce is often a scary, lonely, miserable time for a child—full of stress, insecurity, and confusion. Adults suddenly seem remote. God seems far away. Nothing is certain. In this climate a child's coping skills are taxed to their limit.

SUPPLYING SUPPORT

Ultimately a child's adjustment to divorce hinges on four things: (1) the way parents handle the divorce and interact with each other and the child; (2) the way the child perceives the parents' behavior and the losses and changes brought by the divorce; (3) the child's own inner resources: temperament, trust in God, ability to seek help from others, and so forth; (4) the support the child does or does not receive from others during and after the divorce.

The parents, the child, and other people outside the family unit but within the child's circle of relationships all play a part in mediating the child's adjustment. What happens within the home is far more critical than what happens outside of it. Yet children lacking outside support may cope far less well than they otherwise might. To look at it another way, the less support a child receives at home, the more important outside support becomes. In light of this, I feel strongly that God would have his people play a far greater role in the lives of children of divorce.

What can be done? Happily, a great many things. These will be discussed in the chapters ahead. But first let's take a realistic look at two prerequisites for helping.

Attitudes

Christians view divorce in many different ways. Some feel that divorce is wrong under any circumstances. Others feel that divorce is legitimate only in the case of unrepentant adultery. Still others think divorce is permissible when there has been physical abuse or desertion. Some have added "irreconcilable differences" to that list.

No matter where one stands on the issue of divorce, it is important to remember that the bottom line in every divorce is *people*—adults and children whom Christ loves and for whom he died. As believers it is our privilege and responsibility to love, accept, and extend a helping hand to these people. But many have instead responded with condemnation and rejection. As a result the church is often the last place to which the wounded survivors of divorce turn—or return.

Children especially need acceptance, love, and encouragement when divorce divides their homes. They are virtually always innocent bystanders, not willing participants, when their parents divorce. Even if they strongly oppose divorce, they are powerless to stop it. Through no fault of their own, their lives' paths become littered with debris that God never intended to be there. It is easy for them to trip over the obstacles divorce casts in their way.

The Living Bible phrases Psalm 119:105: "Your words are a flashlight to light the path ahead of me, and keep me from stumbling." As adults, it may be our privilege to walk alongside one or more children of divorce as they navigate their paths. When we manifest the tender, practical, patient compassion of God, we, in effect, "hold the flashlight" for them until they can hold it for themselves.

Understanding

Adults naturally look at divorce from an adult point of view. But before we can help a child, we need to adjust our perspective. We need empathy.

Webster's New World Dictionary defines *empathy* as "the projection of one's own personality into the personality of another in order to understand him better; ability to share in another's emotions or feelings." It is harder to empathize with a young child than with an adult. Yet empathy beckons us to consider divorce through the eyes of a child. How does it feel to him? What does he fear? What is he angry about? What is his behavior saying?

One major difference in the way children and adults cope with divorce may relate to memories. Adults, even those who have been married for many years, can recall life before marriage. So even if they sense that life after divorce will be difficult, adults at least know that it is possible.

Children, however, have no such assurance. They can recall no life without Father or Mother. In fact, just trying to imagine life apart from a parent may be nearly impossible. One of children's greatest natural fears is that of being abandoned and left to fend for themselves. When separation and divorce breathe life into that fear, an unprecedented crisis can occur. For some, life will never be the same again. For many it means

- Remembering your parents' anniversary and then realizing that there is nothing to celebrate anymore

- Spending Christmas with Mom and then having another Christmas at Dad's

- Having to worry about money
- Wondering deep down inside whether you are really the cause of your parents' unhappiness
- Feeling grief and anger
- Giving up your dreams about all the things you had hoped to do together as a family
- Crying yourself to sleep at night
- Wondering if God really cares
- Feeling insecure and worried about the future
- Losing some of your childish innocence and trust
- Praying and pleading and trying with all your might to change the situation, but failing in your attempt
- Wondering if you'll get married when you grow up, and if you'll get divorced, too

Every caring adult in the child's circle of relationships can play a unique role in his or her adjustment to divorce. I once heard someone say, "Life is *relationships*." Both biblical and secular wisdom support that idea. Relating to others brings joy, meaning, and fulfillment to life. Sharing and communicating with other people helps us know who *we* are. Interaction stimulates us intellectually, emotionally, and spiritually. A healthy network of relationships that meets our need for love and acceptance frees us to look beyond ourselves to consider the needs of others.

Unhealthy or broken relationships have the opposite effect. Whether we are estranged from our Creator, a friend, a spouse, or a parent, a broken relationship makes it hard to feel good about ourselves or about life in general. It's hard to think of the needs of others—sometimes just hard to think at all—until there is restoration, forgiveness, and healing.

Life *is* relationships. This is as true for children as for adults, but not in the same way. For children, life is primarily— sometimes exclusively—family relationships. The younger the child, the fewer relationships he or she has formed apart from the immediate family. When family relationships reach the breaking point of divorce, life goes topsy-turvy. Learning to live with, instead of repairing, a broken relationship becomes the task of the whole family. It's not easy because it's not natural.

At this difficult time adult friends can reach out to children with love and encouragement. Children's perceptions of relationships and their trust of adults may have been dimmed by the divorce. Because of this, patience and a warm personal touch—smiles, hugs, a listening ear—are essential in conveying an understanding spirit.

Because life *is* relationships, we must take care not to overly institutionalize our outreach. On one hand, because of their professionally trained staffs and communal resources, churches, schools, clinics, and agencies can do many things that no private individual could hope to do. But on the other hand, personal involvement with close friends, teachers, neighbors, and relatives administers a healing touch that paid counselors cannot provide.

Most children would undoubtedly adjust better and faster if help were available from both qualified professionals and caring laypeople. Ideally, all parties—two parents, the child's teacher, Sunday school teacher, a professional counselor, friends, and extended family—offer informed support and encouragement to varying degrees. But when this does not happen, even one person who is genuinely concerned and willing to listen can make all the difference in a child's life.

Perhaps you can be that person.

2

A Death in the Family

*The death of my parents' marriage has shown
me that the union of a man and a woman is
indeed the creation of a new life. Marriages are
living things. And sometimes they die.*

—Bruce Yoder, pastor[1]

In the original scheme of things, marriages—like men and
women—were not supposed to die. But, in different ways, both
mankind and marriage have fallen under sin's sentence of death.
All people will physically die, whether or not they are prepared
for it, whether or not they consent to it. Marriages, on the other
hand, don't die of their own accord. They are either starved to
death or dealt an intentional death blow by one or both of the
partners. Otherwise, marriages live until the spouses are separated by physical death.

Divorce is the legal means by which husbands and wives
pull the plug on the marital life-support system. To some,
divorce is a mercy killing. To others, it is nothing short of
murder. Either way, the marriage dies, and the children who
mourn its passing are thrust into a no-man's-land of grief: The
marriage is dead, but the parents live. Family members are the
same, but life is very different. Contradictions like these make
divorce one of the hardest griefs for a child to bear.

We usually associate the word *grief* with physical death.
But anything perceived as a loss, big or small, tangible or
intangible, can evoke grief. Denting the fender on a new car,

losing a valuable ring, or missing out on the family reunion—all can cause grief.

The depth of a person's grief depends on how significant the loss is perceived to be. How great was the emotional investment in what was lost? A loss that seems slight to one person may be overwhelming to another. An adult may feel that a child is overreacting to a parental divorce, yet only that child knows how it feels to be the son or daughter of these particular parents and to be losing the things he or she feels are being lost through their divorce.

The Losses of Divorce

Losses, both tangible and intangible, can be incredible. Tangible losses can include:

- The daily presence of a mother or father in the home or in the child's life
- The daily presence of a brother or sister, who goes to live with the other parent
- The family home, which may have to be sold
- Familiar surroundings—a move prompting a change in school, classmates, neighborhood friends, after-school activities, church involvement
- Income—diminished resources mean fewer clothes, toys, family outings, and so forth
- Aunts and uncles, cousins, or grandparents, who will never be seen again
- The after-school or evening companionship and supervision of Mother, who must now work outside the home
- A pet or hobby that can no longer be afforded or made to fit into an apartment lifestyle

Intangible losses are also keenly felt. Such losses include:

- Security
- A stable home environment
- Respect and status in the eyes of others
- Happiness and a sense of well-being
- Trust in adults

- Faith in God

- The ability to concentrate in school

- A sense of being able to control one's own life

- The "mirror" of the absent parent, providing feedback of ideas and behavior that influences self-evaluation

- The identity that comes from seeing oneself as a part of a normal family

- Hopes and dreams of potential family ties and times, even when the predivorce family situation has not been especially positive

Compounded Losses

Beyond these things, a child may feel embarrassed about the divorce, rejected by the parent who left, lonely, guilty, fearful, and confused—all at once.

Many of these losses *by themselves* would be sufficient to produce a period of grief. The fact that these things are happening simultaneously multiplies grief upon grief. That they are happening as a result of parental *choice* to divorce adds insult to injury.

Seen as a package, these compound losses contribute to yet another loss—the loss of self-esteem. In their Loneliness Research Project, psychologists Phillip Shaver and Carin Rubenstein discovered that children of divorce often have lower self-esteem than other children.[2] In her book, *Second Chances*, Dr. Judith Wallerstein wrote that divorce "requires children to overcome the profound sense of rejection, humiliation, unlovability, and powerlessness they feel with the departure of one parent. . . . They conclude that had they been more lovable, worthy, or different, the parent would have stayed. In this way, the loss of the parent and lowered self-esteem become intertwined."[3]

Psychologists tell us that the closer we come to our ideals about how we feel we ought to be or really want to be, the greater our self-esteem. This means that Christian children of divorce may have an especially acute loss of self-esteem. They may have been from a "good Christian family" last year, but now their family is a "bad example." They used to feel loved and accepted by people at church but now may feel shunned and avoided or regarded with suspicion, embarrassment, or pity.

GRIEVING DIVORCE

According to child psychologist Lee Salk, divorce ranks second only to parental death among childhood traumas. "Divorce is, in a way, worse than death," said Patty, forty-four, a divorced mother of two. "Death is a natural part of life; we know it will happen. We never suspect that divorce will occur as we march down the aisle on the wedding day." Children never suspect it will occur either, and, in at least four ways, divorce *is* actually worse than if a parent had physically died.

No Ceremony

To begin with, marital death, unlike physical death, has no socially accepted ritual that eases the grief of the survivors. Joseph T. Bayly has written, "The viewing and funeral are our sole concession to death. As a result, they must bear a heavy weight of grief-expression, death-affirmation and memorialization."[4] A divorce is often as heart-rending as a death, especially to a child. But where is the ceremony that bears the "heavy weight of grief-expression, death-affirmation and memorialization" of the marriage? There is none. The reasons are not hard to comprehend.

Unlike death, divorce is often an embarrassment to the family. Unlike death, it is a choice. And unlike death, the divorcing parties hardly wish to memorialize the "deceased," even though children often feel differently. So there is a death in the family, but no viewing, no funeral, no ceremony, and quite often no fellow mourners to surround the family with understanding and consolation. As a result, the grief a child experiences when parents divorce can be more severe than when a parent dies.

No Clean Break

Physical death, with its funeral ceremony and burial, releases the family to start afresh. First there is grief, then healing, and then closure of the wound. It is over. The person is gone. A new chapter in life begins in which the deceased person has no role except in memory. There is sometimes a sense of relief: "Mommy doesn't have to suffer with her cancer anymore. Now she is with Jesus."

Divorce is seldom like that. There has been a death, but not a total break. Like death the loss is permanent, but unlike death it is only a partial loss. Both parents live and continue to play out their parental roles according to revised scripts. There may be ongoing disagreement about custody, child support, visitation and other issues, making it hard to make a new start.

As children grow older, grief is revived as they make new discoveries of ways in which the divorce has affected their lives. They may grieve afresh at any time, when wounds are reopened. Time spent with a friend's intact family, or the seemingly conspicuous absence of one parent at a special school function, or the annual reminders of Christmas or Father's Day may trigger a new rush of grief.

False Hopes

Divorce and parental death differ in a third way, involving hope. Because the parents have not died, there is always the possibility in the child's mind that they will reunite. Almost every child secretly nurtures a reconciliation wish. Common fantasies are usually variations on the same theme: Mom and Dad realize that they really do love each other after all. They iron out their differences and get back together, and the family lives happily ever after. That this is so universal a response suggests that divorce, like death, was never meant to be.

But even death holds the promise of a resurrection. All who die will live again. Those who have trusted Christ will spend eternity with him; those who have rejected the Savior-Messiah will be eternally separated from God. Children instinctively believe that a dead marriage can also live again. But marital resurrection rarely occurs, and the childish hopes that flourish after divorce are almost certain to lead to disappointment and disillusionment.

In her book *Where Has Grandpa Gone?* Ruth Kopp notes, "Any loss that is expected to be temporary is more difficult to mourn than one perceived and accepted as permanent."[5] The tendency to cling to the ideal of reconciliation hinders children in the important task of grieving.

Isolation

When a family member dies, the rest of the family huddles closer for mutual support and consolation. People outside the family reach out with expressions of sympathy and kindness, assuring the mourners of several things: that it's normal to be feeling loss and emptiness, that their grief is understood and accepted by others, and that they are loved and cared about by a circle of friends and family members.

By contrast, a child whose parents divorce rarely receives adequate comfort from family members or outsiders. In her book *Second Chances,* Judith Wallerstein wrote, "It amazes me how little support they get at this time, even from grandparents. . . . In our study, fewer than 10 percent of the children had any adult speak to them sympathetically as the divorce unfolded."[6]

Many people are understandably reluctant to reach out to a family experiencing divorce. They don't know what to say, and it's hard to know what to do; it doesn't seem right to send flowers or take food the way one would if there had been a death. After all, it's always *possible* that the family may be *happy* about the divorce. Consequently and unfortunately the result is often a complete avoidance of both the people and the problem.

I read about one woman and her son who experienced this reaction. When the woman's first husband had died, her church responded immediately with gifts of food, phone calls, sympathy cards, visits to their home, and other demonstrations of love. Her young son was much impressed and moved by this, as was the woman herself. Later the woman married again, but the marriage was troubled and ended in divorce. After her husband left the home, no one called or came by. There were no gifts of food or encouraging cards or notes. There was only silence. The boy remembered vividly the response other Christians had given when his father had died. Now he had lost a second father and no one seemed to care. It puzzled him greatly. "When will the people from church be by?" he asked his mother. She tried to help him understand that yes, divorce is a lot like death, but it is different, too. In divorce you bear your grief alone.

Because of the dynamics within the family at the time of divorce and the hesitation of those outside the home to become involved, divorce often creates an isolated grief.

And according to fifteen-year-old Sarah, such treatment is painful: "I just don't like being isolated, especially when you know something like a divorce is happening. Acting like we're freaks or we're weird, that we're different now and not normal— I don't like people doing that to me. They just don't know how to handle it. They're scared, I think."

RESPONDING TO LOSS

Grief is a normal, God-given response to loss. In grief, we withdraw to ponder what has been lost. As we comprehend what has happened, we begin to adjust. Slowly we emerge to cope with life again, minus what has been lost. Grief is not only natural, but also necessary. To suppress it, deny it, or defer it is to interfere with emotional healing.

Barbara Spence, a divorced mother of three, discovered that this is true for adults and children alike. She wrote,

> I learned that [my children needed] to be allowed to grieve too. They have lost a part of themselves. Their lives, which had been safe and snug up to this point, were completely uprooted. They are young, but they know that something terribly important has been lost to them forever.
>
> But who allows the children to grieve? So many parents want to "protect" their children by telling them half-truths or vague realities. And it's easy to be so overwhelmed by your *own* pain and guilt that the children and their pain take a back seat. It's tragic and it's wrong, but it happens.[7]

Children need to grieve the losses of divorce. Denying that children have lost anything of value, or refusing to allow them to sort through feelings and experience grief, is detrimental to their emotional and psychological well-being. Those who are not permitted to deal with their losses as they occur will likely confront them again at a later date, perhaps as adults.

Every child has a personal timetable for adjustment. On the way to emotional healing, both adults and children pass through various stages of a grief cycle. Though some experts feel that younger children do not grieve in the same sense as adults, it is agreed that they experience pain in loss. The grief cycle is typically experienced in a sequence:

DENIAL: "This isn't really happening."

ANGER: "Why, why, why?"

BARGAINING: "I promise I'll be extra good, if only . . ."

ACCEPTANCE: "This *is* happening, and I can cope."

GROWTH: "I'm going to be stronger because of this."

Some believe the sequence is a little different, suggesting shock as a first response, followed by denial, anger, self-pity, and acceptance. In more basic terms, any person who sustains a loss can respond in one of three ways: try to avoid it, try to change or undo it, or accept it. A grieving person typically goes all three routes, arriving eventually at acceptance. People progress at different rates through the stages of grief, sometimes repeatedly cycling back through stages before finally accepting the loss.

Avoid It

Avoid it is a typical child's first reaction to divorce because the news is too hard to digest. It really can't be true! Very young children may avoid dealing with the idea of divorce by pretending that the absent parent is at work or on a long trip. This denial functions as a cushion that keeps the awful truth from hurting them. But as long as children continue to deny the inevitable, they can move neither backward nor forward. They cannot go backward because what was no longer exists; they cannot move forward because they have not yet accepted what has become reality. A fantasy of avoidance is not abnormal, and it is usually short-lived.

Change It

Change it is almost always the desire of children who learn that parents plan to divorce. They argue, reason, and plead. They may pray earnestly, perhaps trying to bargain with God. They may become unusually cooperative. But to no avail. Everything is going to change.

In this tumultuous stage, many different feelings and reactions can occur, varying with the age and personality of the child.

Depression. Depression is the classic sign of grief. Depressed children shift into low gear, seemingly to absorb the trauma at a more tolerable pace. They withdraw, preferring to be alone rather than with friends or family. They may spend a lot of time thinking and may cry easily. Their ability to concentrate in school may suffer. They may not feel like eating or may overeat. They may have trouble sleeping at night or may feel constant restlessness during the day. Self-confidence shrinks and decision making becomes difficult.

Anxiety. Anxiety is really a form of fear. Many things that previously felt secure and could be taken for granted now seem uncertain. What is going to happen next? Will people laugh at us? Will Mommy leave me, too? Are we going to be poor? Do I have to change schools?

Anxious children are apt to be very busy children, trying to bury uncertainty and fear in a flurry of activity. They may have nightmares, temper tantrums, and physical manifestations of anxiety, including stomachaches, diarrhea, headaches, asthma, or chest pains. They may begin to bite their nails or wet the bed. They may be afraid to let their custodial parent out of their sight and may worry about that parent getting sick, dying, or otherwise abandoning them.

Anger. Practically every child will be angry about a parental divorce. Because something so dramatic is occurring entirely against their will and outside their control, they will feel frustration and insecurity resulting in anger, a normal part of the grieving and healing process.

Unhealthful anger has two faces: guilt and blame. Guilt can result from anger turned inward: "This is all *my* fault." Anger turned outward results in blaming others for what happened: "Why did *you* let this happen?"

Children who cannot verbally express their anger or are prevented from expressing it may turn to indirect or "passive-aggressive" outlets for their rage. Instead of being open about their anger and finding acceptable outlets for it, these children express it in masked ways such as bad attitudes, disobedience, being critical of others, not doing well in school, or harming pets or property. This kind of anger is not healthy and needs rechanneling with the help of an experienced counselor.

Accept It

In the grieving process the child has been fighting against acceptance of the reality of the loss. It may be a long, hard road for some, but as the truth sinks in—that they can neither run from reality nor change the circumstances—acceptance gradually takes root.

SUGGESTIONS FOR HELPING CHILDREN COPE WITH THE GRIEF OF DIVORCE

1. Allow children to spend time alone but offer to keep them company. For example, a parent, grandparent, or baby-sitter could read or do needlework in the same room as a child without forcing conversation or activity. But the adult might *invite* the child to take part in whatever is going on.

2. Recognize depression as part of a necessary healing process. Be gentle and understanding, knowing that depression can make it more difficult for children to feel motivated and to make decisions. At the same time, it is important to maintain discipline and see that chores and homework assignments are accomplished. Depressed children still need the security of boundaries, rules, and responsibilities.

3. Proverbs 18:21 says, "The tongue has the power of life and death." Build a child up; don't tear down with your words. Name calling and ridicule from a parent stings more than it would from anyone else. Conversely, kind words can

strengthen and encourage. Give verbal support: "I know you really miss your dad. I realize that this isn't an easy time for you."

4. Allow children to talk about the divorce or about an absent parent. This may be trying, but talking can help them accept losses, just as talking about one who is deceased helps family members accept the death.

5. Let them know, above all, that you *accept* them and their feelings. Let them know it's okay to cry and it's okay to want to be alone. Assure them that you're a good listener, should they want to talk. But it's also all right if they don't want to talk. With smaller children, physical comfort is especially important. Holding them, rocking them, tucking them in to bed, or just sitting close by can be comforting.

6. Custodial parents can make changes in the child's environment and lifestyle slowly. The fewer changes that confront children simultaneously, the less overwhelmed they will feel. For example, postpone moving to a new neighborhood or going to work for the first time, if possible, for as long as you can.

7. Excessive anxiety, unhealthy anger, or prolonged depression may call for professional help. A parent who is experiencing prolonged grief or depression will probably benefit from therapy as well. This will help children in the long run, too, since hurting parents find it hard to be sensitive to their children's needs.

8. Encourage adult friends not to avoid the subject of divorce but to show their concern and lend a listening ear.

PART TWO

HOW CHILDREN RESPOND TO DIVORCE

Introduction

This section details the way children react to divorce. Though every child is a unique individual facing a unique set of circumstances, in a general sense we might say that all children respond similarly; children tend to blame themselves, experience fear, feel rejected, angry, and lonely.

Yet a closer look reveals that a child's ability to comprehend divorce and deal with its stresses varies according to his or her age. Understanding the probable responses of each age group is a first step toward helping a particular child.

The following chapters will be most useful when seen as an overview of possible common responses rather than as an attempt to stereotype children of divorce at their various stages of development.

Long-term research on children and divorce has recently illumined an interesting fact: A child's initial response to divorce does not necessarily predict that person's eventual adjustment.[1] It appears that many factors combine over time to shape the overall effect of divorce on a child's life. For any child, much depends on how quickly parents regain their emotional stability, how well or how poorly they continue to relate to each other, and the degree to which each of them maintains a positive, affirming relationship with the child.

3

Babies and Toddlers

My five-year-old was only ten months old when the separation occurred. How or if he has been affected, I cannot surmise.
 —Patty, forty-four, single mother of two

THE PREGNANCY DIVORCE

At first thought it seems almost impossible that a baby still in the womb could be affected by a parental divorce. Yet because the two are physically connected, whatever affects the mother can affect the baby.

Divorce may cause an expectant mother to experience a variety of intense emotions, which can change her bodily chemistry. She may be alternately depressed, fearful, anxious, angry, or grief-stricken. Research reported by Linda Francke indicates that the stress transferred from a mother can cause fetal activity to increase as much as 300 percent. Prolonged high-level stress can cause premature births and low birth weights; the babies may have trouble sleeping, may cry more, and experience digestive problems.[1]

Separated or newly divorced mothers with unhappy babies need a great deal of emotional and tangible support from others if they are to make a good adjustment to their mothering role. Friendships are invaluable at this time. Many studies have proven that "supportive social networks facilitate a positive mother-child relationship.''[2] According to one study, ''Mothers with more supportive networks presumably have more of their emotional needs met and thus are better able to meet the emotional needs of their children.''[3]

BABIES

Babies whose parents divorce are affected in several ways that may not be readily apparent. Their earliest life experiences may differ from those of other infants. But what these babies do not experience may actually be most significant.

Father-Care

Virtually all infants will remain in their mothers' custody following divorce. As a result infants usually do not experience routine care and play from their fathers.

Fathers' patterns of interaction with infants are measurably different from those of mothers. Men have deeper voices, wear different kinds of clothing, have larger and more muscular bodies, and actually respond differently than women to babies. Infants of divorce often miss out on masculine nurture and the benefits of two complementary kinds of stimulation. Studies have shown that

- Fathers are "significantly more likely" than mothers to "rock, vocalize with, and imitate" their babies.

- Fathers tend to play in more physically stimulating ways with babies than mothers do. By contrast, mothers tend to play in a more intellectual style.

- Infants respond differently to fathers. One study showed that "infants' response to play with their fathers was significantly more positive than their response to play with mothers."

- Fathers provide more tactile stimulation, while mothers provide more verbal stimulation.

- Fathers who participate in the early care of their infants may experience the same sort of bonding with the baby that is known to occur between mothers and babies.[4]

Babies who receive care exclusively from their mothers and other women, which is often the case following divorce, do not benefit from a father's distinctively different style of care.

Breast-feeding

Another benefit often removed from babies of divorced parents is long-term breast-feeding, which seems to benefit a baby. Breast-fed babies are less likely than others to suffer from colic and stomach upsets. They catch fewer colds and develop fewer allergies, ear infections, and dental problems. Nursing enhances facial development and lessens a baby's urge to thumb-suck. A breast-fed baby is more likely to feel secure and to cry less than a bottle-fed baby due to the positive effects of close physical contact with the mother.[5]

The relative merits of breast- versus bottle-feeding are certainly subject to any mother's circumstances and personal preferences. The point here is not to unduly exalt breast-feeding but to suggest that the stress of divorce may interfere with a woman's ability to succeed at breast-feeding or her desire to attempt it.

Mother-Care

Studies have shown that mothers who do not have supportive husbands tend to behave differently toward their infants than those who do. Not only do these babies miss a father's masculine care style, but they also may experience a different sort of mothering. Studies indicate that

- An encouraging and supportive husband enhances a mother's "sensitivity and adaptation to the needs of the infant."

- Mothering "skills and warmth in handling the baby" have been related to the "anxiety level, age, and marital satisfaction" of the father.

- Both the father's attitudes about the pregnancy and the mother's perceptions of his emotional and physical support have been "consistently correlated with . . . the mother's involvement and responsiveness with the child" throughout the first four years of life.[6]

- "When mothers were with their husbands, they were more likely to explore the baby and smile at the baby than when they were alone with the newborn."[7]

- Parental conflict fosters "less warm and empathic mother-child relationships."[8]

Daytime Nurture

Most of these same infants are likely to experience institutional day care or care from a sitter rather than care at home from their mothers during the workweek. Of course many babies are placed in the care of others by married, working couples. The point is, again, that the single working mother often has little choice in the matter.

While day care remains a hotly debated issue, research accumulated over the last decade identifies extensive nonmaternal care during the first twelve months of life as a "risk factor."[9] Babies receiving more than twenty hours of substitute care a week are more likely to form an insecure attachment bond with their mothers. Insecure attachment has been linked to later negative behaviors such as disobedience and increased aggression.[10]

Divorced working moms often feel trapped: If they don't work, how will they support their children? If they do work, how can they avoid placing their babies in substitute care?

The issue of substitute care is important because during his first year a child develops basic life perspectives that are either trusting or distrusting. The depth of a child's emotional relationship with his primary care giver has a tremendous impact on the formation of this basic outlook on life.

When a baby's cries bring the desired food, cuddling, or dry diapers, he or she quickly learns that actions bring reactions. As a result, competence, security, and trust develop. But when cries make little difference in the way one is cared for, a baby learns that actions do not bring reactions; according to research, these babies actually cry more often than those who are frequently tended. Dr. Paul Chance has summed up the issue by saying, "A responsive environment . . . inclines a child toward competence, while an unresponsive environment inclines a child toward helplessness.''[11] Single mothers who must work, then, need to find an emotionally warm, responsive caregiver for their babies.

At home, divorce and its accompanying depression and stress sometimes make it hard for a new mother to provide a highly responsive environment for her baby. Physically and emotionally drained, she may sometimes feel as much like crying as her baby does. She may find it difficult to put her own feelings aside to concentrate on her baby's needs. Yet her ability to nurture and respond largely determines the kind of bond that will exist between mother and baby.

Authorities on child development believe that a baby's first emotional attachment forms the basis for all of the child's future relationships. Through the mother-baby relationship, especially, the child learns how to give and receive love and how to relate emotionally to another person. Those who are frustrated in this first emotional attachment with their mothers may have trouble with subsequent relationships. To the extent that divorce reduces the mother's physical and emotional accessibility, it can interfere with the mother-baby bond and is cause for concern.

Children who can form attachments to both parents seem to have the greatest social advantages later in life. Psychologist Henry Biller writes, ''Our observations have suggested that children who are able to form strong attachments to both their mothers and fathers during infancy have more positive self-concepts and success in their interpersonal relationships than children who have only an attachment to their mother.''[12] Divorce at this early stage hinders attachment to fathers; after divorce it takes an especially committed dad to build a father-child relationship that starts at the cradle.

TODDLERS

Between a child's first and second birthdays the basic developmental task is that of learning self-confidence. At this stage children become little explorers, investigating, climbing, and poking their noses into everything that captures their interest. Too much interference and thwarting of their natural curiosity and desire for independence may serve to undermine their self-confidence, rather than building it up.

Sometimes emotionally hurting parents want to cling to small children as a security blanket in the wake of a divorce. The adults' own emotional neediness or the fear of losing the children through a custody dispute may cause them to stifle the children, rather than to free them to discover and explore the world. This toddler period is critical to children's intellectual and social development; stimulation from all sorts of places, things, and people is very important. Researchers for Harvard University's Preschool Project found that "providing a rich social life for a twelve-to-fifteen-month-old child is the best thing you can do to guarantee a good mind."[13] They also discovered that those permitted to explore the living areas of their homes freely progressed faster than those who were restricted.

Toddlers are still very attached to Mom and experience anxiety when separated from her. In fact, although children vary in their developmental rates, it is common for them to experience such separation anxiety until the third year or later.

AND NOW FOR THE GOOD NEWS ...

New research has some good news about very young children whose parents divorce: It appears likely that in the long term they adjust very well, compared with children who are older at the time their parents divorce.[14] Babies and toddlers retain little or no conscious memory of those traumatic days, and growing up with divorced parents may be less painful since these children have no way of comparing life before and after divorce.

SUGGESTIONS FOR HELPING
BABIES AND TODDLERS

1. Expectant mothers need extra emotional support during divorce. In many ways, this is a "crisis pregnancy" and professional counseling may be helpful. Expressions of love, concern, and tangible support from others can be invaluable.

A woman who is separated or divorced during pregnancy may need a patient listener, a shoulder to cry on, or very practical help like getting the nursery ready or finding a Lamaze coach. Any ministry to the mother is ultimately also of benefit to the infant.

2. Infants and toddlers need a consistent, familiar environment. The ideal arrangement would be for one reliable, nurturing person, rather than many different people, to care for the child in the absence of the mother, preferably in the child's own home.

3. Even very young children can sense the emotional tension in a divorcing household. Since babies and toddlers will comprehend little from verbal explanations about divorce, seek to comfort them with positive nurturing experiences. For example, spending extra time with them—cuddling, rocking, holding, and playing with them—will help increase feelings of security.

4
Preschoolers
(Two- to Four-Year-Olds)

People don't understand that divorce is very hard on the children and that most children feel terrible the rest of their lives.
—Benjamin, age ten

Preschool children, like babies and toddlers, have an advantage over older children when their parents divorce. Their age at the time of the breakup effectively buffers the effects of divorce in several ways.

Parents and others typically seek to shield young children from the unpleasantries of divorce that older children may witness. And, because preschoolers still need so much physical care and supervision, they often receive more nurture and attention than older siblings during this time. Since preschoolers have most of their childhood ahead of them, they are less likely to be affected by the breakup than older children, who will retain a "before divorce" and "after divorce" frame of reference. These older children may later recall the period surrounding divorce with great and painful emotion, while those who were preschoolers may retain little or no memory of it.

Judith Wallerstein discovered that children of divorce who had adjusted best (ten years after divorce) had been preschoolers at the time of their parents' divorce. She reports that, psychologically, "sixty-eight percent are doing well, compared with less than 40 percent of the older children."[1] In the long term, having been a preschooler at the time of divorce may be a blessing.

But in the short term, there is a great *disadvantage* to being a preschooler at the time of divorce: More than any other age group, preschoolers are frightened by divorce and respond the most dramatically.

One reason for such a strong reaction has to do with preschoolers' dependency on parents, quite literally, for physical survival and emotional security. From deep within, divorce arouses a natural fear of abandonment—a powerful and scary feeling for a young child. And the sense of having been abandoned while young and vulnerable can persist into adulthood. Consider Marcie's experience.

Marcie was three years old when her father left. One of her earliest memories is of waving good-bye to him as he boarded a train. She never saw him again. For years she was plagued with a nagging sense of rejection. Why hadn't he come back? What had she done to make him want to leave? Why didn't he love her anymore? Only after prolonged therapy as a thirty-three-year-old woman was Marcie able to realize that it was not her, but her mother, whom her father had rejected. When the feelings of guilt lifted, Marcie wept with relief.

A TIME OF CONFUSION

Young children like Marcie have trouble verbalizing their deep concerns and questions about divorce. Divorce can be a time of great mystery and frustration as fact and fantasy swirl together in their thoughts: Did Daddy simply disappear, the way things do in cartoons on TV? Is he hurt or sick or hungry? Does he have a place to sleep at night? Such concerns, which seem almost silly to adults, can cause preschoolers to worry. To prevent anxiety, parents should purposely tell preschoolers what is happening. After all, it is quite logical for children to wonder where the other parent is and why he or she no longer comes home at night. Unfortunately, according to one study, 80 percent of the preschoolers whose parents are divorcing are given no explanation of any sort.[2] One of the two most important people in their lives has seemingly vanished, and no one even brings up the subject!

MOM, DAD, AND FEELING GUILTY

Young children tend to perceive their parents as practically perfect: If there is a problem, it cannot be my parents' fault; it must be my fault. Preschoolers also tend to view life in terms of good and bad. Their rationale is likely to be "Mom and Dad are getting a divorce because I've been so bad." In an attempt to reverse the situation, they may try to become super well-behaved even though they may feel guilty and depressed.

Dr. E. Mavis Hetherington, who has done research on children of divorce, feels that preschoolers are prone to self-blame because they have such limited contacts outside their own homes and families. Their whole world revolves around family relationships, so they can easily assume that they are to blame for the family's breakup. They also typically harbor the fear that another family member will leave them.[3]

If a preschooler has fleetingly wished any disaster upon a departing parent, the child's guilt may multiply. Small children believe that their thoughts are powerful. If they think it, it can happen. An angry wish that Daddy would just go away, followed coincidentally by his departure, can be interpreted by preschoolers in only one way: The wish came true!

When the same-sex parent leaves, a child's guilt may be intensified and complicated by his or her developing sexual identity. During the preschool years, a boy often falls in love with his mother, and a little girl with her dad. These tiny romantics are forming mental models of the kind of person they will someday marry. It is perfectly natural for them to wish that their "competition" would just disappear.

In intact families this stage resolves itself quite naturally. But divorce interferes with this resolution in a big way. What was once just a safe fantasy wish has become a scary reality. Little boys left alone with their mothers or little girls left with their dads have no idea how to handle the "romance" once the parent who served as a buffer is removed.

Nine times out of ten, it is the father who leaves the home. This is one reason preschool boys have a more difficult time with divorce than preschool girls. A boy may be guilt-ridden to think that he has actually won out over his father, as evidenced by his dad's departure.

Deep inside, the victory is anything but sweet. He knows he can never take his father's place, and he really doesn't want to. He wishes desperately that Dad would return.

A boy may also feel confused about his masculine role and the kinds of behaviors he is supposed to display. After all, how is he supposed to learn how to be a man when there are no men around? Consequently some preschool boys adopt a somewhat feminine style of behavior modeled after Mom. Henry Biller reports, "The boys who became father-absent before the age of four had significantly less masculine sex-role orientations than those who became father-absent in their fifth year."[4]

Mothers sometimes unknowingly aggravate this problem by discouraging their sons from such boyish activities as wrestling and climbing trees; they give approval for passivity and encourage quiet indoor activities such as reading, watching TV, or coloring. Recently divorced mothers may naturally grow a bit more cautious, eager to ward off accidents and injuries. But by safeguarding their sons' physical safety, they may be contributing to an even greater problem psychologically.

There can also be problems if mothers criticize and tear down their ex-husbands in front of their sons. Little boys know that they are males like Dad, and comments such as, "Men are so disgusting," or, "Men are all alike," will be taken to heart by the child, causing him further insecurity about his masculinity.

A preschool girl has a different problem. When her dad leaves, she feels jilted. Feeling frustrated and rejected, she may strongly deny that her father has left. She may boast of her father's love and frequent attention. Judith Wallerstein found that preschool girls tend to fantasize about being loved by their fathers because this helps them in "undoing the rejection and in maintaining the self-esteem and sense of their own lovability that was threatened by the father's departure."[5]

Girls who visit with their fathers after divorce can be quite hurt by negative comments from their dads about women in general. "Women are stupid" translates into "Daddy thinks I am stupid!" Since their fathers are still the objects of their affections, this wholesale rejection of their sex can be crushing. In the Wallerstein study, little girls whose fathers made caustic comments like these cried all the way home after each visit.[6]

REGRESSION

Preschoolers sometimes regress when their parents divorce. That is, for a time their development appears to go backward instead of forward. Life has become confused, and the energy that should be applied to maturation is focused on responding to trauma. A child who has been independent and pleasant may become a clinging vine who whines and cries a lot. Those who are quite capable of feeding themselves may want to be fed or opt for fingers rather than forks. Thumb sucking may resume. A child who is potty trained may suddenly forget where the bathroom is during the day and wet the bed at night. Physical coordination and the ability to learn may regress, too.

When divorce takes place with relative civility and the household quickly regains much of its former equilibrium, regression does not last long. But when life remains in turmoil, with hostility seething between parents, some aspects of regression can linger as long as a year. Adults can help a regressive preschooler by providing reassurance and getting emotionally involved with the child.

SEPARATION ANXIETY

Preschool children are still prone to feel anxious about separating from Mom or Dad, making visitation a traumatic experience. Steve told me how visitation affected his three-year-old: "When she would come back, she would be terribly upset, almost to a point of being out of control. Of course since she was as young as she was, you couldn't reason too much with her, because she couldn't understand why she had to leave one and live with the other."

Brandon, another single parent, regularly observes this separation anxiety in his preschoolers. "I can see it in the kids each time that they visit their mother and then have to come back to me. I don't know if the words 'torn apart' are exactly the right words to use, but it's like they're torn in different directions. When they go to her, they're being pulled away from me, in a sense. They go through that *every* time they visit."

MODEL BEHAVIOR

Sometimes children who feel responsible for divorce become compliant and well-behaved. Hoping to somehow atone for the crayon marks on the wall that must have made the parent angry enough to leave for good, a child will suddenly become a model of good behavior. This child is, in fact, miserable, but the adults in his or her life are usually more than grateful for the newfound "maturity." Their dead-wrong assumption is that the divorce must have somehow been beneficial to the child, whose behavior has only improved since the breakup. The truth is, the child believes that if bad behavior sent the parent away, good behavior might just bring the parent back. Adults can help unburden a too-good child by repeatedly emphasizing that he or she had nothing to do with the parent's decision to leave.

OTHER RESPONSES

Other responses typical of preschool children include bouts of fear, bad temper, crankiness, anger, or frustration. Some begin to sleep fitfully, probably linked to a fear of being abandoned by the remaining parent. Many of the youngest children in the California Children of Divorce Project displayed a generalized emotional neediness. They reached out for attention and affection from any adult at all, even climbing into the laps of strangers.

After his wife left, Brandon noticed an increase in moodiness in his two preschoolers. He soon learned to take this as a cue that their "emotional tanks" were getting empty and they needed increased attention from him.

> Usually when I sense this—sometimes it takes a while to catch it—I'll just cancel something for an evening. If I was going to be home that evening anyway to work on stuff at the house, I'll just push it all aside and spend the whole evening with them. And it makes a world of difference in them. It really does.

Anger is part of the mourning process. Girls are more likely to turn their anger inward, blaming themselves; boys tend to turn anger outward, blaming others. Both may be confused about why they feel as they do. Inward anger may be manifested when the child deliberately does things to harm herself or make herself uncomfortable, perhaps as punishment for causing the divorce. Outward anger includes aggressive or bullyish behavior, which can harm relationships with peers.

Interestingly, as bullyish behavior subsides, girls tend to be welcomed back into their circle of same-sex peers, while boys often continue to be ostracized and unforgiven. The boys' only recourse may be to play with girls or younger children, which fosters immature behavior. Mavis Hetherington feels that during the second year following divorce, boys who have had this problem might benefit from a move to a new neighborhood or school. With their adjustment period past, they can make new friends and leave their bad reputations behind them.

PLAYTIME

Anger and fear have a way of showing up in the way a child plays. Because young children are so unskilled at expressing themselves verbally, they will often act out feelings using dolls or puppets or in their play with peers. Observing the way a child plays can be very revealing. Inventing disasters such as fires or monsters that attack the play scene may be safe ways for a young child to express how it feels when parents divorce.

Adults can help children tap into their feelings by using dolls or puppets that talk about feelings. For example, the adult's doll could say to the child's doll, "I cried when Daddy left, 'cause it made me feel so bad."

Artwork is also telltale. The way a child portrays himself, his family, and his home may provide clues regarding personal feelings about divorce.

Music, too, can stimulate a child to express feelings. Sandy recalled how music helped her daughter open up for the first time. The song "Just When I Needed You Most" by Randy Vanwarmer was on the radio when she and her daughter were driving home one day. One line in the song says, "Where I'll find comfort, God knows, 'cause you left me just when I needed you most." Sandy said, "My daughter sat in the car crying. She said, 'Why did my daddy have to leave?' In over a year that was the first emotion she showed; she had buried it so deep down."

SUGGESTIONS FOR HELPING PRESCHOOLERS

1. Use the read-aloud story at the end of this book to help preschoolers identify their feelings and fears about divorce. Listen carefully to their comments and questions and respond with concern. Make positive eye contact when you use the discussion questions to engage the child in conversation. It may be best to read only one chapter at a sitting; take your cues from the child's level of interest.

2. Every preschool child needs a simply worded verbal explanation concerning divorce. Ideally both parents should talk to the child together before the actual separation takes place. It is important to use language that preschoolers can understand. Words like *custody* or *visitation* are probably meaningless to them. They need to know basic information such as where they will live and how often they will see their other parent. Preschoolers have a limited concept of time, so, again, it is important to speak their language.

3. Provide repeated assurances that the child is in no way responsible for the breakup. Parents might say something like, "I know you feel bad about the divorce, but the problem is between Mommy and Daddy. Divorce is a grown-up

problem and it has nothing to do with you. The divorce is not your fault.'' (Chapter 2 in the read-aloud story at the end of the book is intended as a resource for helping children see that they played no part in the parents' decision to divorce.)

4. If the father has left the home and does not maintain an adequate involvement with the children, surrogate role models are important, especially for boys. Trustworthy male relatives, Sunday school teachers, and friends can provide positive examples.

5. Spend a generous amount of quality time with the child. Physical affection—hugs, stories read on the lap, tucking in to bed at night—warmth, positive eye contact, and genuine attention communicate love and acceptance.

6. Refrain, and ask others to refrain, from making negative, critical, or condemning statements about the child's other parent when the child is present.

7. If possible, take the child to see where the noncustodial parent is living soon after that parent leaves the home. This way the child will see that the parent has a safe place to live, a bed, and food, and is in no danger. Preschoolers are reassured by this and can also visualize the parent's home from that point on.

8. The parent who moves away from the family residence can, with some effort, maintain a close relationship with preschoolers.

5
Five- to Eight-Year-Olds

What upsets me most about my parents' divorce is the hurt that you get down deep.
                                    —Candace, age eight

For most children, the transitions and challenges of the early school years are pleasant. The years from five to eight are treasured as relatively carefree, serene, and happy. When divorce occurs during this rather idyllic period, it can cast a long shadow on the children's ability to be happy and on their sense of well-being.

SADNESS AND DISILLUSIONMENT

When parents divorce, children often experience a parent's departure from home as rejection. Children in this age group, more than any other, experience overwhelming grief when their parents divorce. Dr. Wallerstein noted that deep sadness was "the most striking response" of these early elementary children, and described them as "more intensely conscious of their sorrow than any other group in the study."[1]

Many five- to eight-year-olds respond with panic, sobbing, and great fear when their parents separate. A comment by Gordon Livingston, director of psychiatry at the Columbia

Medical Plan in Columbia, Maryland, is especially descriptive when applied to this age group. He said,

> The disillusionment that comes with the knowledge that your parents do not love each other anymore and are not going to stay together is probably as profound as the eventual knowledge that someday you are going to die. It's not only a tremendous blow to a child's conception of the world as an orderly place, but it shakes his fundamental faith in everything. It's the one thing children expect to persist and when it doesn't, it's scary.[2]

COMMITMENT TO FAMILY

Most early elementary children tend to remain unswervingly devoted to both parents, no matter how much attention or inattention they receive, or how much one parent may pressure the child to renounce the other. Children of Divorce Project researchers felt that about a quarter of the five- to eight-year-olds in their study were being pressured by their mothers to reject their fathers. They commented, "These youngsters continue to be loyal to both parents, frequently in secret, and often at considerable psychological cost and suffering. Their capacity to do this, despite the pressure, and their courage were often moving and impressive."[3]

Few children at this age are capable of being angry with their fathers, but some, especially boys, direct strong anger toward their mothers for supposedly driving their fathers away. As a rule, being angry with either parent is hard. Social reasoning at this age tells them that you can't be mad at somebody and love him or her at the same time. This is evident in peer relationships: I'm mad at Cynthia, and I'm never going to be her friend anymore! Relationships are pretty much all-or-nothing-at-all. So being mad at Dad or Mom makes little sense because it might mean risking the loss of that parent. And that is the very last thing five- to eight-year-old children want.

What they *do* want—fervently—is a reunited family. Being with one parent then with the other but never with both can be quite dissatisfying. They want both parents, and they want them together. As a result the reconciliation fantasy is strong.

Seven-year-old Greg, whose family was the subject of a TV documentary on divorce, is typical. He told his interviewer, "I want them back together no matter what. I'm never going to give up."[4] Eight-year-old Mary Beth told me, "I wish my mother would get married to my dad again. I want them to get together and not stay apart." But of course fairy-tale reconciliations rarely occur, and holding onto the fantasy only strengthens and prolongs a child's grief. The desire to reunite Mom and Dad also makes kids resistant to the idea of parental dating. Boyfriends or girlfriends of either parent are a direct threat to the cherished dream of reconciliation. Verbal or nonverbal efforts to deter or at least dampen parental dating can be anticipated.

FATHER-LOVE

Children this age, especially boys, characteristically display an intense yearning for their noncustodial fathers. It is not uncommon for a child to feel abandoned by him. Authorities on divorce and children have observed that boys have an especially difficult time if they are the oldest child or the only boy in the family. Many have difficulty concentrating in school and may become hostile or aggressive. Boys whose fathers exit their lives become father-hungry and are eager to accept father substitutes, seeking out male teachers, neighbors, and others in an attempt to fill the void. Such boys typically overinvest in the relationship, creating the potential for disappointment should the prospective father-figure not be attentive.

Mothers who date a succession of men should be aware of the potential effect on their sons. A boy who becomes emotionally attached to a series of boyfriends only to have them fade out of the picture may become disillusioned and learn to shrink back from making emotional commitments. His ability and desire to form future good relationships may be hampered in the process.

Girls feel the loss of Dad too, but they are less willing to accept substitutes. Their affections still belong to Daddy alone. They willingly cultivate relationships with adult males and enjoy their attention, but they rarely make a strong emotional investment in potential father surrogates. Instead, when Daddy pays little attention, a girl compensates by fantasizing about his love and devotion to her.

Fathers who are not regularly involved with their five- to eight-year-olds may not realize how desperately their children desire a relationship with them. One third-grade girl told me, "My father needs to understand that I want him home more than anything in the whole world." Many of the children interviewed in the California Children of Divorce Project longed for their fathers with an intensity reminding researchers of grief for a dead parent.

Research indicates that if a father does remain involved with his children after divorce, he is likely to devote more attention to his sons than to his daughters. Five- to eight-year-old girls can be deeply hurt by a father's inattention and seeming preference for their brothers. The ache of having felt rejection from the first and most important man in their lives can color future relationships with a sense of being unlovable.

FEARS AND RESPONSIBILITIES

Whether grounded in reality or not, fear plagues many children after divorce. The fear of losing the custodial parent is common. One of their biggest concerns is that the parent will replace them with a new spouse, another child, or even a pet.

Children who are unable to talk to their parents about their feelings may be especially prone to unrealistic fears, such as a fear of starving or a fear about going to school.

Eight-year-old Mary Beth dreads that "we might drive off a bridge." She has other worries, too. "It scares me," she says, "when I think that my mom might marry someone mean." Candace, who is also eight, says she gets scared just thinking about her father. She admits, "Sometimes I worry about him coming back and hurting us."

Children who have been told by well-meaning adults that they are now "the man of the house" or "the little homemaker" may be fearful about their ability to take the place of the departed parent. Custodial parents who are depressed or emotionally unstable are most likely to usher the child into this unrealistic role, grateful for the comfort it brings them. Other parents think it's cute when a little boy assumes his father's place at the dinner table or when a little girl tries to take over as family cook. Children, of course, cannot adequately assume adult roles and can be filled with anxiety in trying.

Overworked single parents may be tempted to allow their children to assume as much responsibility as they are capable of, both in caring for themselves and in taking care of the house. First and second graders may be given the responsibility for getting themselves up on school days, fixing their own breakfast, packing their own lunches, and making sure they catch the right school bus at the right time. After school it is up to them to get home safely, let themselves into the house, and amuse themselves until Mom gets home. They may be expected to see to the needs of younger brothers or sisters, perhaps making their supper and putting them to bed. And they may be responsible for a number of household tasks.

Children in these situations are apt to feel neglected and angry that they are not cared for the way their friends are. Some hardly see their parents, who may work odd hours, moonlight, take night classes, or date in the evening. Children who have no siblings may spend many lonely hours at home by themselves.

Even the busiest single parents need to keep in mind that children need supervision, guidance, and nurture, if not from parents, then from parent-substitutes who can free the children from enough of their duties and concerns to allow them to enjoy childhood. Household tasks assigned to children should not merely unburden a parent, but should be chosen to help children feel more competent and important. Jobs they can succeed at in a measurable way are best because they will boost their self-esteem. By contrast, jobs that are beyond their capabilities ensure their failure or frustration, making them feel discouraged and incompetent.

FEELING DEPRIVED

Five- to eight-year-olds are deeply affected by the many tangible and intangible losses they sustain through divorce.

Feelings of deprivation are not unusual. As a result, some become compulsive overeaters, trying to fill the emotional void with food. Grieving losses on all sides, others compensate by demanding more material possessions—often more than parents can afford to provide. They say they need new clothing, toys, athletic gear, and gadgets that their friends have. When their wishes cannot be fulfilled, some children respond by making up stories about possessions they don't really have or lavish vacations they have never taken.

Feelings of deprivation can make children selfish with the things they do possess. Perhaps feeling that they cannot risk the loss of one more item, they can become stubborn about sharing with others. Feelings of deprivation can even tempt children to help themselves to some of the more desirable items in a friend's possession. The line between what belongs to "me" and what belongs to "you" becomes blurred in an all-out effort to make the empty feelings go away. Author Linda Francke wrote, "Feelings of deprivation are symptomatic of the anxiety these children feel about the impermanence and the inadequacy of their family support systems. All they see around them is loss— of a parent, of parental attention, of extra money, of a secure future."[5]

SUGGESTIONS FOR HELPING
FIVE- TO EIGHT-YEAR-OLDS

1. Use the read-aloud story at the end of the book to help younger school-age children identify their feelings about divorce. Listen carefully to their comments and questions and respond with concern. Make positive eye contact when you ask the discussion questions and engage the child in conversation. Those who are able to read may want to read the story themselves and then discuss the questions with you.

2. Five- to eight-year-old children are apt to perceive a parent's departure from home as rejection. The parent who leaves can take steps to maintain a close relationship with the children following divorce. Fathers especially need to bear in mind

how much their sons need to feel loved by them. Fathers who have both girls and boys should guard against the tendency to show preference for sons over daughters.

3. Assure children that they are loved and that they will have adequate material provision. Pray with them about family needs and their personal needs. Let them observe your reliance on God for both material provision and emotional strength.

4. Never pressure children to renounce their loyalty to either parent. It is entirely normal for them to care for both parents, and they are in fact under biblical mandate to do so—"Honor your father *and* your mother" (Exodus 20:12; Ephesians 6:2, italics mine). Attempts to turn children against one parent are likely to backfire anyway. At some point children will come to resent the person who pressured them rather than the parent they were supposed to have turned against.

5. Don't feed the reconciliation fantasy. In almost every case it is kinder to remind children gently that their parents are divorced and that this is a permanent arrangement. Tell them that the parents' decision to stay apart is final. (Chapter 4 in the read-aloud story may help a child better understand the finality of divorce.)

6. Do some special things from time to time to help take the sting out of feelings of deprivation. Simple and inexpensive gestures can go a long way toward increasing feelings of security. Here are a few ideas:

   - Tuck a special "I love you" note into a jeans pocket or lunchbag.
   - Surprise the child with a batch of warm chocolate chip cookies.
   - Send a greeting card through the mail. (Most young children don't get much mail!)
   - Give a small, inexpensive gift for no reason.
   - Take the child to McDonald's for Saturday lunch.
   - Add a slight increase to the child's allowance.

7. Help children cultivate wholesome and rewarding friendships with adults who can in some measure be surrogate parents or positive role models.

8. Do not encourage children to try to fill the role of the parent who left the home. When others imply that this is something a child should now do, temper these comments with assurances that the child does *not* have this responsibility.

9. Custodial parents who cannot be at home when their child comes home from school can arrange for a sitter or relative to be there, or work out an arrangement so the child can stay with a neighbor or at the home of a school friend until they arrive. This companionship not only assures greater safety for the child, but also helps ward off feelings of loneliness and isolation, particularly for an only child.

6
Preteens
(Nine- to Twelve-Year-Olds)

*I think divorce is terrible and that parents
shouldn't be able to do it.*

—Benjamin, age ten

The physical and emotional developments of preteens
significantly influence their response to divorce. Around the age
of nine, children develop more mature coping skills, allowing
them to understand that the rift between their parents is
something for which the children are not responsible. They are
the first age group able to point out ways in which divorce may
have benefited their parents, although they are anything but
pleased about what Mom and Dad are doing to the family unit.

Nine- to twelve-year-olds are still family oriented with a
strong sense of family identity. They scrutinize parental behavior
and values, subjecting them to typical preadolescent black-and-
white thinking. Socially, preteens have had time to build a solid
base of support outside the family and develop a string of
achievements in various areas that help boost the self-esteem
that divorce threatens.

In many ways it would appear that preteens are in a
position to weather the storms of divorce successfully. Yet
divorce at this stage in a child's development can be traumatic in
entirely different ways than for younger children.

Recent research reveals that in the long run divorce takes

its greatest toll on kids who experience it during their preteen and teen years. These older children may not recover as well as those who are younger at the time of divorce.

There are several reasons for this. First, older children go through normal developmental stages of identifying with and separating from their parents. When divorce complicates this process, the child experiences difficulty. Second, older children have often had longer exposure to an unhealthy marriage and to marital conflict. Researchers now believe that, whether it occurs during marriage or after divorce, intense, unhealthy parental conflict is damaging to children and is linked to behavioral and academic problems.[1] When divorce comes late in a conflicted marriage, children have already lived for years in a difficult environment.

These children may be confused about what makes for a healthy relationship. As a result, many experience difficulty in their own relationships and find it hard to make commitments. As the years go by these children may struggle not so much with the divorce itself as with what went on in the home before the divorce.

ANGER

Even when there is conflict in the home, preteens are not likely to welcome divorce. The most characteristic preadolescent response to divorce is anger.

"It's not fair!" preteens cry when they think that someone is not playing by the rules. Divorce calls forth anger because it breaks all the rules about how parents are supposed to behave. Black-and-white thinking does not allow exceptions to the rules, and the rules, both biblical and secular, say that you're supposed to stay married to the same person. You're not supposed to get involved with somebody who is not your spouse. You're supposed to set a good example for your children. If you're a Christian, you're supposed to forgive each other instead of getting a divorce. So nine- to twelve-year-olds are embarrassed, outraged, and humiliated when parents break the rules—rules the parents themselves may have imparted. If children feel that one parent is particularly at fault, the anger they feel may be directed especially at that person.

This view of divorce is aggravated by feelings of power-lessness, prompting anger to spill over into relationships with peers and parents. At school anger may be reflected in the quality of work and in behavior. Friends may be alienated just when they're most needed. Both parents may be targeted. When anger is directed at the visiting parent, visits become unpleasant. Fewer visits may result, making the child even angrier.

Wallerstein and Kelly felt that anger at this age is linked to the removal of the father from the home. The father is generally perceived by children as the parent whose presence governs discipline, impulse control (the ability to refrain from doing things he knows he shouldn't do), and delay of gratification (the ability to wait with desires that are more properly fulfilled at a later time). When Dad leaves, children may feel a "sense of moral indignation and outrage that the parent who had been correcting their conduct was behaving in what they considered to be an immoral and irresponsible fashion."[2]

Preteens are often embarrassed by divorce and try to hide their home life from others. On the outside they can appear cool even when they are seething on the inside. In response to both their anger and embarrassment, these children often lose themselves in a flurry of constructive or destructive activity.

ALIGNMENTS

Because these children tend to cope through vigorous activity, those who are emotionally vulnerable can be incited by one parent to turn against the other parent in a hostile or vindictive way. This unhealthy parent-child relationship, called an "alignment," fits in nicely with preteen black-and-white thinking. The child can easily be persuaded that the parent with whom he or she is aligned is the good parent and that the other is the bad parent.

While the stated purpose of a parent-child alignment is often that of restoring the marriage, in reality its purpose is to inflict misery and retribution on the former spouse. The "good" parent may enlist the child to spy on, harass, or humiliate the "bad" one, all the while fueling the child's indignation.

When alignments occur between a custodial parent and a child, the child is usually a son and the mother is the custodial parent. When the alignment is between a noncustodial parent and a child, it usually involves father and daughter.

One of the most unfortunate aspects of an alignment is the damage it can do to the excluded parent. His self-esteem may be shaky after the divorce; on top of that, his own child is employed against him as an agent of ill will. Often this parent attempts earnestly to establish a positive postdivorce relationship with the child—who is unable to view him apart from the distorted and hostile perspective of the alignment.

In terms of children, alignments are particularly destructive in their long-term effects. Judith Wallerstein noted that within five years after a divorce almost all alignments had disappeared. But for boys in particular, unresolved preadolescent anger endured into the teenage years, manifesting itself in unhealthy behaviors, including theft, drug use, arson, and promiscuity. Some of the teenagers generalized the anger they had felt toward their parents so that it now encompassed all adults or the world as a whole. In contrast, others were able to confine their anger to the still-excluded parent, enabling them to do well in school, make friends, and live successfully.

When parents have not sufficiently reconciled to the point of speaking face to face, children are sometimes employed by both sides to deliver threats, to spy, to report back on the activities over at the enemy camp, and to keep secrets from each parent. Jonathan feels that his son and daughter are angry because "for a long time they were 'used' by both parents in what they already seemed to understand was a selfish, vengeful effort to win their affection. They knew we both loved them so much, but they would rather have been somewhere other than in the middle of the conflict." Brenda, a divorced mother of two, similarly observed, "My children are angry that they are the victims of their dad's anger and are often used as a buffer or communicator between their dad and me."

One eleven-year-old tersely summed it up: "In a way I hate

them both. What they've put on me. What they talk to me about."[3]

Clearly, as with almost everything else about the divorce, the preteen feels strongly that their being used as a pawn is *not fair*. Mental health experts identify children caught in a long-term war between two hostile parents as high suicide risks.

LITTLE ADULTS

Nine- to twelve-year-olds can competently do laundry, go shopping, care for younger children, or cook meals—duties gratefully relinquished by busy, tired, or depressed single parents. Children in this age group, especially girls, may be given a disproportionate share of chores, even when there are other children in the household. Said twelve-year-old Kim,

> It's harder on me because there are only two of us to do the housework. If Mom were there all day she could get it done, but she has to come home from work and get it done. My brother, if my mom asks him, will clean up the kitchen, and sometimes my sister will fold the towels, but mostly my mom and I will do it.

A 1991 study of fifth through ninth graders in the Chicago area revealed that children in single parent homes actually spend about the same *amount* of time as other children in household and maintenance type tasks. But since most of these tasks fall to custodial mothers, the study showed that when they were spending time with their mothers they were more likely to use that time for maintenance tasks.[4]

Preteens may be able to carry an adult's share of the work, but the fact that they are still children shows up in their worries: What if Mom is killed in a car accident? What if she gets sick? What if she loses her job? Preteens are not equipped to face life without the security and provision of a parent, and the prospects of having to do so can be frightening. Those who come home to empty houses, eat supper alone, and go to bed in a house that is spooky-quiet can easily become fearful and lonely.

Children who see little of their parents not only take physical care of themselves, but they also parent themselves with regard to decisions, values, and goals. A child's morality, philosophy of life, and personal goals may be founded on the wisdom of peers, the media, and the child's own best judgment. Yet preteens actually want parental guidance and the security of discipline and boundaries. They need rules to live by and parents to model after. They also want to have a meaningful relationship with their parents—knowing what they think, what they feel, what they believe. And they want to be known by them in the same way.

But time for serious parent-child discussions about moral and spiritual values is next to nonexistent in many households. After working a full day a single parent must tend to the necessities of life—grocery shopping, paying bills, taking the car to be repaired, mowing the lawn, dental appointments. Where such conversations do take place, parents deliberately carve out time in the family's schedule to tend to their children's character development and emotional and spiritual needs.

Some parents make little adults out of their children in another way—by depending on them excessively for emotional reassurance, comfort, and support. Such children can feel responsible to take care of that parent and may feel guilty about leaving him or her in pursuit of their own interests. In a role reversal with the parent, children lay aside age-appropriate activities to tend to the hurting parent. This makes it very hard for children to achieve one of the developmental tasks of preadolescence, that of beginning the break with childhood.

Everything about the preteen is pointing toward increased independence. The social life is picking up; intellectual horizons are expanding; even hormones are hinting that childhood is becoming a thing of the past. But a child who feels the burden of parenting a parent will have trouble breaking away. The child may feel torn and resentful. When adolescence finally arrives, such a child may find it impossible to make the necessary break from a dependent parent.

THE RECONCILIATION FANTASY

Ben is ten years old and lives in Louisiana; Paul is twelve and lives in Pennsylvania; nine-year-old Tim lives in Florida. I asked each of them to complete the same sentence any way they wanted. Their answers leave no doubt that the reconciliation fantasy is alive and well at this age.

BEN: If I could, I would "get my mom and dad back together."

PAUL: If I could, I would "make it so Mom and Dad would get back together."

TIM: If I could, I would "get them together again."

Kimberlee, age twelve, knows of an honest-to-goodness real-life reconciliation of the sort that would spark hope in any preadolescent. She related, "A friend of mine up at school, her parents got a divorce, but they found that they couldn't live without each other. He said he didn't love her anymore, but he really did. They got a divorce, but they got back together 'cause they still loved each other."

While children at this age fervently desire a reunited family, they are also able to temper their desires with reality. Paul, for example, admitted that realistically "there is a slim chance that they'll get back together." Ten-year-old Paige said that she would tell other kids to keep a hopeful attitude because "they might get together or they might not." Her personal outlook is not so bright, however. She explained matter-of-factly that her own dad "can't come back because he's married to a lady."

SEXUAL TENSION

Preteen girls are beginning to mature physically. Many a father, divorced or not, finds himself pulling back from his daughter at this time, as if in self-defense. He is no longer quite sure how to treat this daughter-turning-woman. Daughters need reassurance about their femininity and lovability during puberty, and Dad's pulling back causes frustration and self-doubt.

Eleven- and twelve-year-old girls have an especially strong need to feel approved by their fathers. Dr. Ross Campbell has said that paternal approval is "absolutely essential" if a girl is going to feel self-approved in her feminine role.[5] Divorce often takes fathers and daughters even further apart than usual since the awkwardness felt on both sides can be heightened by infrequent contact.

A daughter who feels somewhat distant from her father is apt to feel jealous when he begins to date. Seeing Dad with someone other than safe, comfortable Mom illuminates a disturbing fact: Dad is a sexual being. This fact is normally masked in intact homes and is something that most preadolescents would prefer not to think about. As a result, daughters often strongly dislike—even show hostility toward—the women in Dad's life. Said one daughter, "When he saw us he would bring his girlfriend along with him. That upset us like crazy. I could not stand it." Experts say that the period between a child's ninth and fifteenth birthdays is the worst time for a parent to remarry. The child and stepparent are likely to be at odds, and sexuality figures prominently in the discord.

If a girl knows or suspects that her unmarried father is sexually active, the tension between her and the adult parties can grow even worse. She is apt to lose respect for him, hold his partner in highest disdain, and refuse to visit him when the woman is present or when she will be spending the night.

Having to confront parental sexuality at a time when her own sexuality is beginning to blossom complicates a girl's puberty. She can become excessively focused on sex, perhaps becoming sexually active herself. Dr. Wallerstein observed that many children of divorce "used sex to shut out anxiety and to ward off a sense of emptiness and depression, and they started early. Over a quarter of the girls became sexually active in junior high school and have continued their sexual activity ever since."[6]

SUGGESTIONS FOR HELPING NINE- TO TWELVE-YEAR-OLDS

1. Parents, do not draw your child into an alignment against your former spouse no matter how angry you may feel and no matter how justified you believe you are. Seek professional help if your anger is eating at you, but don't feed your child's anger with your own.

2. Parents, remember that preteens are still children. Don't allow them to become overburdened by asking them to support you emotionally beyond their capabilities. Instead, console them in their worries about your welfare. Talk about what would happen to them if you had an accident or if you were to become ill. Make provisions in your will for their custody and care, and discuss what kind of finances might be available for their college education, wedding, and so forth. If these are unresolved issues, take steps that will put them to rest for both you and your children. You may need to consult a lawyer or confer with your former spouse.

3. Parents, personally teach your child God's standards of morality and discuss the ways these conflict with the standards of our culture. If you feel ill-prepared for this task, enlist the help of a pastor and/or Christian therapist. Ask them to suggest resources. Remember that while others can provide guidance, this is a parental responsibility. It is critical that your words and conduct do not conflict with each other. Preadolescents are not only listening, but also watching. Seek out spiritual guidance for yourself if you are confused about these issues. If the child's other parent is promiscuous, model and teach biblical morality, but do not verbally condemn him or her.

4. The involvement of fathers is still of vital importance. Boys need them as behavioral models, and girls need their affection to feel self-approved. At least initially, fathers of preteen girls should try not to involve women they are dating in their visits with the children.

5. Don't use your children as informers regarding your former spouse's lifestyle or activities. Don't use them to carry messages back and forth between parents. Do your own talking and work hard to keep the lines of communication open.

6. Parents who lead especially busy lives need to take time to be alone with individual children. Make time to talk about important issues, such as values and goals, as well as mundane happenings. A habit of daily conversation is best.

7. Keep in mind that children read actions louder than words. First John 3:18 tells us how to let them know that they are loved: "Our love should not be just words and talk; it must be true love, which shows itself in action" (TEV). Dr. Ross Campbell's fine book *How to Really Love Your Child* (Victor Books) is an excellent resource.

7

Teenagers

I wish my mother would understand that it's hard on us kids and not just her.

—Anna, age seventeen

The teen years mark the passage from childhood into adulthood. During the early teens boys mature physically. Both boys and girls become socially oriented, with a keen interest in the opposite sex. Each year is different from the last, bringing new challenges and new steps toward independence.

When the slow process of emancipation and maturation is finally drawing to a close, both parent and child breathe a sigh of relief. The teen years can be stormy and tumultuous in any family, but especially so for families undergoing divorce. Parental divorce—whether it occurred recently or long ago—is a variable that makes adolescence all the more complex.

As noted previously, new research indicates that older children—those who are preteens and teenagers when their parents divorce—often have more long-term divorce-related difficulties than younger children. Here are some of the issues involved.

IDENTITY

Teenagers are on a quest to secure their personal identity. Both parents and their backgrounds are probed for clues that might help answer the "who am I" question. Teens want to discover their heritage—religious, ethnic, social, genetic, and otherwise.

A recent divorce forces a teen to make adjustments to his own long-standing identity and to his sense of family identity. There may be an identity crisis even when divorce occurs after a child is grown. Bruce Yoder was finishing college when his parents divorced. He asked, "Had I come from a happy family or not? I used to think so. So too did everyone who knew me as I was growing up. But if the family was happy, why was there a divorce to contend with? What was real?"[1]

If a teen has identified closely with a same-sex parent, divorce may also challenge his or her self-image. A recent divorce also forces a teenager to reevaluate his beliefs about commitment and relationships. The fact that parents who used to love each other no longer do offers proof that even the most well-intentioned commitments aren't necessarily forever. Moreover, the very people he thought he could always count on to be the same have now changed dramatically in their relationship with each other. He may wonder if he is destined to reenact his parents' divorce one day.

Teens whose noncustodial parents walked out of their lives may feel an almost instinctive urge to locate those parents, much as adoptive children search for biological parents. Feelings of rejection may resurface.

Adopted children may especially struggle with feelings of rejection. Kids who have always secretly wondered why their biological parents gave them up for adoption may now experience the awful sensation that history is repeating itself. Now it seems that one or both of the *adoptive* parents aren't sure they want an adopted child either. One adopted fifteen-year-old told me why she believed her parents had divorced:

> Basically, my father wanted a child of his own, of his own flesh and blood, and he didn't want adopted children. He felt that only a

child could give him something he didn't have. So he went off and had an affair with this lady. She became pregnant. After a year of separation my parents divorced.

Whether the divorce was recent or long ago, teens may scour old photo albums, scrapbooks, and yearbooks, asking questions designed to produce evidence that their parents' love was once real and that their children were loved and wanted. If possible, wise parents will furnish proof and assurances that this was the case, realizing that teens need this as a bolster to their own future relationships.

Parents are sometimes mystified when a teenager digs through the ruins of the marriage. Equally baffling are the simultaneous changes in behavior. Christian counselor David Martin told me:

> It's because now they've put the pieces together. Now they're finding out: "It wasn't all mom's fault or all dad's fault and somewhere in the picture I've got to find out where I am as a person." And that's rough! It's hard enough trying to change gears from childhood to adulthood with a growing healthy family, let alone having to deal with a malfunctioning one.

SECURITY

Sixteen-year-old Angela said, "I think divorce is good for people that can't communicate and live a normal life. I'm happy that my parents are divorced rather than living with the stress and resentment." Jennifer, age seventeen, said, "Divorce is not right, but sometimes necessary."

Even though teenagers like Angela and Jennifer are more likely than younger children to view divorce as a reasonable solution to serious marital problems, many also feel strongly that their parents are selfish for pursuing divorce at this stage in the teenager's life. Why not wait just another few years, until the child has left home? Why add more complication to a teen's life at a time when it is already more complex than he or she ever imagined it could become?

Without question, the most significant way that divorce

complicates a teenager's life is by knocking out the supports of home at a time when they are needed in a critical way. Teens normally progress toward adulthood by taking two steps forward into the unknown and sometimes frightening process of growing up, then one step back toward the safety and security of home and parents. With the knowledge that home and family are always there if needed, teens edge their way little by little toward their destination: independence. Divorce complicates emancipation by crumbling the security of home and forcing the child to plunge into the real world all at once.

In her first book chronicling her research, Judith Wallerstein stated, "The toppling of the family structure at this time burdens . . . normal developmental processes and threatens to derail them. The adolescents who came to us felt that the change in the family had limited or entirely removed the family as a safe base for refueling."[2]

In her second book, after a decade of research, Dr. Wallerstein wrote, "It is worth repeating the fact, which seems largely underestimated by the American public, that children need an enormous amount of support during adolescence. The children of divorce say it over and over again. We should listen to them."[3]

Girls, she found, are especially vulnerable and "have a particularly strong need for family structure during adolescence."[4] Boys, she said, "experience a rising need for their fathers during adolescence—even if the divorce occurred ten years earlier."[5]

Brett, fifteen, complained, "It hurts–we haven't seen him for two years. I've played the guitar for five years and he's never heard me play. And he hasn't called us for our birthdays or Christmas, sent us a card or anything!"

Many teens with divorcing parents suddenly find themselves taking a back seat to the family's turmoil. Mom and Dad are more wrapped up in their emancipation from each other than in the adolescent's emancipation from them. In this climate of benign neglect, some teenagers allow immaturity to rise up in protest. Feeling adrift, without family supports intact, some are incapable of resisting the lure of the streets. A recent study found that "children who experienced parental divorce during

adolescence were more likely to be involved in substance abuse
. . . than were children who experienced no divorce or a divorce
during their preadolescent years." Another study found that
boys were more likely than girls to use drugs after the divorce.[6]
Some teens turn to promiscuity for escape and solace. Others
drop out of high school; twice as many dropouts come from
divorced homes as from intact homes.

As the family unravels, teenagers often feel a conflicting
sense of loyalty to both parents. Divorce breaks the marital unit
into separate entities in separate households, often with differing
sets of standards, rules, and requests with which the children
must comply or fall into disfavor.

Some kids strive to please both parents, even to their own
discomfort. Sixteen-year-old Bob told me that "trying to live up
to both their standards and expectations" was one of the hardest
things about the divorce. Some, like seventeen-year-old Jennifer,
have decided which parent has which rights. Her father hasn't
been able to get the picture though. She said, "I wish my father
would understand that since he doesn't live with us anymore he
has given up some of the rights a parent has—like making
rules." Other teens completely give up trying to obey and please
two parents, figuring, *If I'm on my own (as I seem to be),
parental wishes and demands simply don't matter much anymore.*

ANGER AND GRIEF

As we have seen, anger is a stage of grief. Teenagers of
divorced parents acutely feel the losses of divorce. They may not
recognize that their emotional responses—bad dreams, difficulty
in concentrating, depression, feelings of emptiness, and chronic
fatigue—are part of the grieving process. They may just know
that they are miserable, angry, and feeling sorrow and loss.

A divorce that took place in years past is now significant in
new ways. As teens look back at their childhoods with nostalgia,
they may suddenly feel angry if their memories do not include
happy times with both parents. They may feel they missed out on

something they should rightfully have had or be upset that parents did not try harder to resolve their differences.

When divorce forces young teens to grow up almost overnight, they may mourn the death of their childhood along with the death of the family. They may deeply resent the fact that their parents' needs have upstaged their own and left them feeling alone and unable to rely on family. The inability to do anything to put the family back together further angers and frustrates them.

In her book *Which Way Is Home?* Leslie Williams described her feelings of anger as a college student whose parents divorced:

> This volcano of anger! Where does it come from? This is shocking. I didn't know I had so much hostility inside me. Now that I start thinking about it, I realize I am mad because our family has broken up. I am angry because our parents couldn't work out their problems, angry because I am unhappy and miserable on account of something that isn't my fault. . . . The nights are still bad. I'm still having bad dreams, and I wake up sometimes with my fists clenched and my heart pounding. I simply do not know how to handle this anger, this unfocused stream of emotion. How do you handle being angry at a 'situation'? You can't talk to a situation or hit it, or get back at it, or change it in any way.[7]

The sources of teenage anger in a divorce situation are as varied as the households from which teenagers come. Jennifer is angry that she cannot relax and be herself around either parent. She says she always has to "be careful what I say to one or the other of them because if there's a problem, my dad blames it on my mom or vice versa."

Angela is upset that her father "expects me to communicate to Mom for him."

Fifteen-year-old Sarah is especially angry that her father lied about the affair he was having. He is now married to the other woman, who is expecting his child. The sight of her bulging tummy, says Sarah, "just makes me mad."

Angry teenagers can sometimes be pulled into an alignment with one parent against the other. But most parent-teen alignments dissolve rapidly, perhaps because an older child can see virtues as well as flaws in both parents. Or perhaps it is because teenagers more often want to please both parents and feel conflict when they deliberately alienate one and give preference to the other. A teenager under pressure from one parent to turn against the other is likely to resolve the dilemma by backing away from both parents, allowing the anger on all sides to cool.

This backing away is a common response, and one that seems to have value. In the Children of Divorce Project study, teens who had been close to their families before the separation and those who had been emotionally distant were both observed to pull back from the conflict at home. The divorce served to push into total independence those who had already been distant. Those who had previously been close were initially a source of concern for researchers: Were they becoming self-centered and uncaring about others? But one year later researchers were pleased to see that the withdrawal had seemed to be beneficial. They reported,

> Creating distance from the parents at the height of the struggle saved these youngsters from overwhelming anguish, humiliation and emotional depletion, and enabled them at a later date . . . to be supportive, empathic and sensitive to needy parents. Thus their withdrawal served to maintain the integrity of their development.[8]

SEXUALITY

Most teenagers are vitally concerned about their ability to relate well to the opposite sex. Sex itself is a monumental concern, occupying much of their thought life. Divorce frequently heightens a teenager's preoccupation and anxiety about both sex and dating.

One of the first surprises many teenagers have after their parents divorce is the sudden youthfulness of their formerly outdated parents. Mom and Dad may begin to wear more youthful clothing and hairstyles or speak teenage jargon. In the starting-over mentality that often follows divorce, a parent may be grappling with the same issues as the teenager: Who am I? What is my purpose in life? What are my standards for relating to the opposite sex? Is sex outside marriage okay? Instead of having stable, reliable parents who could guide them through these same issues, many teens find that parents are asking the same questions they are—while leaning on them and competing with them on their turf.

In the lonely and confusing aftermath of divorce (particularly in the second year), many adults seek out sexual encounters. Some, of course, are sexually involved even before the marriage ends. Teens are bound to be aware of either parent's sexual activity.

The younger the teenager, the more apt he or she is to be upset by the knowledge that a parent is engaging in sex outside of marriage. Some feel almost betrayed, responding with disgust and embarrassment. Others use the stumbling block of parental immorality to rationalize sexual involvements of their own.

Studies have shown that teenagers from divorced homes are more likely than other teens to become sexually active—at a younger age and with more partners. Some are perhaps seeking warmth and physical comfort as a diversion from the problems at home. Others may be subconsciously trying to start a family of their own to replace the one that has fallen apart. Girls may unwittingly continue the search for the love of a father who has long since chosen not to be an affectionate and involved part of their lives.

EXPECTATIONS

In the shadow of their parents' failed marriages, many teens come to expect failure in their own relationships with the opposite sex. Many of the teenagers in the Children of Divorce Project took it for granted that they would fail in marriage and as sex partners. The researchers in this study described the outlook of these teens as an "unquestioning acceptance" of the fact that these failures would characterize their lives. In interviews conducted ten years after parental divorce, researchers found that every child was afraid he or she would repeat the parents' failure.

Almost as if living out a self-fulfilling prophecy, many teenagers from divorced homes are unable to maintain long-term dating relationships. Some, fearing the loss of yet another person they care for, become overly possessive, demanding far too much loyalty and suffocating the relationship. Others, finding that long-term relationships make them uneasy, move from one relationship to another, preferring to end a friendship rather than resolve a conflict.

Most of the teenagers who shared personal divorce experiences with me saw the need to proceed with caution toward marriage and were apprehensive about their chances for a successful and lasting relationship. They were painfully aware that the odds for any marriage are not especially encouraging today. But having observed their parents' mistakes, they want desperately to succeed. Here are some of their comments:

JENNIFER: It scares me when I think that one out of two couples gets divorced. For me as a Christian, divorce is not an option. However, it will be difficult for me, because of my parents' divorce, to try and remember that divorce is not an option. I am afraid that when my husband and I have a fight I will think that the only solution is divorce. This feeling comes from seeing my father get married and divorced three times.

BRETT: Divorce is definitely wrong. When you get married, you commit. You say you'll stay together for the rest of your life when you take the vows. Plus all that it says in the Bible. I don't know if I'm really scared of being married, but it could happen to me too. But if I have kids, I don't want my kids to go through what I'm going through. I'd try everything not to let it happen. 'Cause it's not fun.

ANNA: I worry about the future. It really scares me. It scares me when I think about my marriage and whether it'll be a success. When I get married someday, I will make sure that our love is true and pure and make sure it will last forever.

ANGELA: Someday I plan to get married and use my parents' marriage as a guideline so my marriage will turn out to be happy and fulfilling. I will be sure that there is good communication in my family.

BOB: Someday in the near future I'll get very close to a girl. When I get married I will have a good *loving relationship*.

SARAH: I pray about my marriage now. It's something I didn't do before. But I pray about it now—that God will give me the right person to live with and spend the rest of my life with.

CAROL: I think divorce is the most emotionally painful situation a child can go through. I will never put my kids through a divorce if I can help it. When I get married someday I want it to be the perfect marriage—full of love, honesty, and trust.

BOYS AND GIRLS REACT DIFFERENTLY TO DIVORCE

Until relatively recently, it has been thought that, overall, girls adjust better to divorce than boys: In almost every measurable area, girls have appeared to fare better than their brothers do. But researchers now believe that boys and girls are both significantly impacted, but that they respond in different ways and at different times.

Researchers now understand that boys, especially, tend to externalize, or act out, their distress, and that they do so *following* divorce. Girls, on the other hand, are more prone to internalize their distress and are thought to be more sensitive to their parents' distress before divorce. Boys may have appeared more affected simply because more research has focused on measuring behavior after divorce. A few-year study of adolescents found that "girls showed their negative consequences prior to the separation and did not appear to decline further after the divorce. . . . For boys, however, the main consequences appeared to occur after the divorce."[9]

As researchers have had the opportunity to follow the children of divorce over time, they have also been surprised to discover what Judith Wallerstein has termed a "sleeper effect" in young women, but not in young men.[10]

The sleeper effect is basically a delayed reaction to parental divorce. It seems to come into play some time after high school, when a young woman is on the verge of adulthood, often as she seeks to enter into a serious relationship with a man. At this point she may be overwhelmed by depression and anxious fears about betrayal, abandonment, and rejection. Some young women also seek out sexual relationships with older men, as if in search of their father's missing affections. According to Dr. Wallerstein's research, this sleeper effect is laden with potential disasters because it occurs at the very point in a young woman's life when so many crucial decisions are made concerning marriage, career, and family.

Both British and American studies have found that girls from divorced families are more likely to divorce as adults. American women with divorced parents have a divorce rate sixty percent higher than for the general population.[11] A study by two University of Texas sociologists showed that "white women who were younger than 16 when their parents divorced or separated were 59 percent more likely to be divorced or separated themselves."[12] This study also indicated that all children of divorce are apparently more prone to divorce than those from intact homes.

Because the sleeper effect appears to be common—two-thirds of the girls in the Wallerstein study experienced it—[13] and because it comes at a pivotal point in life, it seems wise to suggest professional help for young women who have struggles relating to the parental divorce.

LEAVING THE NEST

Divorce has few admirable aspects, but it can bring beneficial maturity and wisdom to some teens. Those able to learn from their parents' experiences are likely to view marriage as a serious undertaking and to think about the qualities that build good, workable relationships. The teen who allows divorce to serve as a tutor will give careful thought to financial responsibility, morality, career choices, and other important concerns.

As a teenager gets close to the time when he or she will

leave home—for college, to take a job, or to get married—guilt about leaving the custodial parent may rise up accusingly: She needs you. How can you leave her? Considering this nagging thought, many older teens would be happy to see their parents remarry. Unlike younger children, they are concerned about how their aging parents will cope financially and how they will handle the loneliness of growing old without a spouse. Many would welcome a stepparent and view him or her as a parental companion and a source of economic help. As Angela said, "My mother needs to understand that there is nothing wrong with building another relationship and starting life over."

SUGGESTIONS FOR HELPING TEENAGERS

1. If possible, provide reassurance that parents at one time did love and care for each other and that the child was wanted and loved by both of them. Photographs depicting the child with both parents are tangible evidence of this. Such keepsakes can help the teenager build confidence that his or her future holds the promise of a happy marriage and family.

2. Parents, work hard to "be there," realizing the importance of home and family during this final phase of childhood. Keep open lines of communication but refrain from pouring out your own problems and frustrations to teens. Adults need to find other adults in whom they can confide. Teenagers, however, should be encouraged to talk their concerns over with parents or other adults.

3. Try to change as little as possible following divorce in an effort to help teenagers feel more secure. Moving out of the family home, changing churches, beginning to date, and even redecorating the house can be approached slowly so teens are not confronted with too many changes at once. Involving teens in decisions surrounding these choices will help them understand reasons for changes.

4. Young women in their late teens and early twenties who are having a difficult time due to the "sleeper effect" would likely benefit from counseling with an understanding therapist,

preferably someone experienced and trained in childhood trauma issues.

5. Dr. Ross Campbell's book *How to Really Love Your Teenager* (Victor Books) is an excellent resource.

PART THREE

TELL ME WHERE IT HURTS

8
Report Card Blues

I think divorces are terrible and they make me cry.

—Mary Beth, age eight

Divorce commonly affects a child's ability to perform in school. Many exhibit a marked inability to concentrate and an increase in daydreaming. Two-thirds of the children in the California Children of Divorce Project showed notable changes in the way they behaved and performed in school after their parents' separation. More than half were seen by their teachers as highly anxious. One-quarter were extremely preoccupied with the problems at home, and about 20 percent were felt by teachers to be experiencing "considerable sadness and depression." This sadness, daydreaming, and difficulty in concentration caused one-fifth of the students a "significant decline in academic achievement during the several months following the separation."[1]

In general, the more chaotic the household, the more difficult it is for a child to concentrate in school. Eight-year-old Candace observed, "The hardest part about having divorced parents is *thinking* about them." What are the children thinking about? Research shows that girls spend a great deal of time trying to come up with ways to reconcile their parents. Boys tend to worry more, especially when one parent is depressed.

EMOTIONS

Some children respond to the pressures of divorce by throwing themselves into their schoolwork as if their lives depended on it. For some this may be almost true in terms of emotional survival. By immersing themselves in their studies, they are able to insulate themselves from the pain that would otherwise preoccupy their thinking. These are the students who seem to have an innate ability to hold their grades up in spite of their gnawing emotions.

Sarah, a high school sophomore, managed to keep her grades high amid bouts of depression and sorrow over her parents' divorce. She asserted,

> You can get through it. It's not the end of the world, and it's up to you to make it not be the end of the world. It's only you that decides whether you're going to allow your grades to fall and get you down or go on and live each day in a new way. Basically, it's up to you.

Yet she freely admitted,

> You know, there's just some days still that I just get so involved in it and it hurts me so bad that I can't concentrate in school. The only reason I'm there is I know I have to go on, no matter where I am and what kind of mood I'm in. I remember a day this year when I was so bad in biology class that I said to the teacher, "Look, can I go to the bathroom? I just can't sit here any longer." And I've had several days like that this year.

During divorce children may experience a whole barrage of emotions ranging from fear and insecurity to depression and despair. The intensity of what they feel may vary from day to day according to the way the drama at home is being played out. Add to this the possibility that they may not have shared their feelings with anyone else at all, and it is not the least bit surprising that school performance may ebb and flow with the family's ups and downs.

James Dobson has said,

> *Emotions affect the efficiency of the human brain*. Unlike a computer, our mental apparatus only functions properly when a

delicate biochemical balance exists between the neural cells. This substance makes it possible for a cell to "fire" its electrochemical charge across the gap . . . to another cell. It is now known that a sudden emotional reaction can instantly change the nature of that biochemistry, blocking the impulse.[2]

This is most likely to occur, says Dobson, "when social pressure is great" or "when self-confidence is low." A child may experience either or both of these during divorce. And lowered school performance can lower self-esteem and self-confidence.

Paul, a seventh grader, has trouble handling his divorce-related anxieties. His mother said, "Paul's grades have dropped since he has been in the custody of his father. He's gained a lot of weight also. Paul feels that it is his responsibility to look after his dad and to take care of him. I think Paul is unhappy." Paul knows that his burdens follow him to school, but he doesn't know what to do about it. He confided, "It scares me when I think that my seventh grade report has very low grades."

Fifth-grader Ben feels much like Paul. Ben is still sorting things out a year after his parents' divorce. He lamented, "I have lots of pressures, and it is hard to complete school work and do practically anything."

Children who must move to a new school shortly after divorce may find that their grades are additionally challenged as they try to cope with their personal problems amid new teachers, new classmates, and an unfamiliar building and curriculum. The newness of their surroundings may complicate their inner struggle by introducing a sense of loneliness or isolation.

Anger can contribute to falling grades. Unable to verbalize what is bothering them, children may communicate anger passively by failing in school, even though they are capable of better work. Studies through the years identify "family in-tactness" as a major factor relating to whether or not a student drops out of school. One study observed that "students from broken homes are not likely to find the support and encouragement they need to keep them in school."[3] Those who do stay in school are "40 percent to 75 percent more likely to repeat a grade and 70 percent more likely to be expelled from school."[4]

The good news is that most children are able to resume

good academic functioning after they have gone through a period of adjustment. Children of Divorce Project research showed that at the five-year mark following divorce, three-fifths of the children observed were doing average or better-than-average work in school. The majority were excellent students. Another quarter of the children in their study were achieving below average. Only 16 percent were doing poorly. Interestingly, these low achievers included a large number of thirteen- to-sixteen-year-olds, the same group who, five years before, had been intensely angry about their parents' divorce.

Further good news, according to this same research, is that once the bulk of the crisis is past, kids start to like school again. Half of the children interviewed in the California Children of Divorce Project disliked school at the time their parents separated. One year later two-thirds again had positive feelings about school.

LINGERING EFFECTS

Even when divorce is amicably and quickly resolved, it may leave its mark on a younger child's ability to learn in certain areas. There are two reasons for this. The first relates to a child's living with only a male or female parent instead of with both. Men tend to excel in analytical, mathematical, spatial, and mechanical skills. Women tend to be most proficient in verbal ability, language, and perception of detail, such as in reading. Exposure to only one set of these sex-related skills can possibly influence the way a child learns.

Children of divorce tend to score lower as a group in math and subjects that require problem-solving abilities. This may be due to the lack of paternal influence, since nine out of ten children are in the custody of their mothers after divorce. Boys tend to be more affected academically than girls, perhaps because they lack a male model to pattern their cognitive skills after. Boys who have brothers tend to be less affected than those without brothers. Yet psychologist Henry Biller found that a mother can significantly influence her sons academically by her attitude. He wrote, "Poor school adjustment among father-absent boys was associated with their mothers' negative attitude toward their absent husbands."[5]

Girls can also be affected by Dad's absence from the home. Biller found that "father-absent girls have often been found to perform more poorly on intelligence and achievement tests than father-present girls."[6] In addition, a positive correlation has been found between a girl's verbal ability and the amount of reading she observes her father doing. Daughters of divorce often cannot benefit from their father's example—because Dad is no longer at home when he reads.

The second reason divorce may influence a child's ability to learn has to do with the disorganization that often characterizes a postdivorce household. Divorce researcher Mavis Hetherington feels that in a highly disorganized household a young child will have difficulty developing a long attention span. Problem solving requires the ability to concentrate for long periods, and a child who does not develop this ability will suffer academically. Once again, Henry Biller links this to the absence of the father: "Academic success requires the capacity to concentrate, delay gratification, and plan ahead. These abilities are less likely to be well-developed among paternally deprived children than among well-fathered children."[7]

Children who gain a stepfather soon after divorce seem to have an advantage in their intellectual development. Biller reports one study that found that "father-absent children who had a father-surrogate in their home (i.e., stepfather) did not have intelligence test scores that were significantly different from father-present children. These findings can be interpreted in terms of a stepfather presenting a masculine model and/or increasing stability in the home."[8]

IN CLASS

Teachers have observed that for many children, Monday is a bad day. Some are still feeling the disappointment of a visit that was promised but never materialized. Others are in the process of adjusting to a change in location, perhaps having arrived home late the night before from a weekend visit with their noncustodial parent. Similarly, Friday can be a day of confusion for those who leave directly from school for a weekend with one parent or the other. Did I remember to pack everything? Is Dad picking me up? Or is Mom? I can't remember!

Teachers who observe the following kinds of behavior in their students may be wise to interpret them as possible clues that parents may be in the process of divorce. Specific suggestions for teachers are included in chapter 15.

Nodding off to sleep in class. Sometimes children become so scared or insecure after a parent leaves the home that they sleep only fitfully or try to stay awake guarding the house. Often they force themselves to stay awake when a parent goes out for the evening, even if a sitter is present, fearing that the parent will not return.

Dropping grades or failure to do homework. Previously good students may become depressed or anxious to the point of being unable to concentrate on schoolwork, either in class or at home. Poor students may begin to do even worse. Confusion at home may also contribute to the failure to do homework.

Changes in behavior. Some may become bullies, suddenly domineering or aggressive. Some just have trouble getting along with classmates. Others may become uncharacteristically quiet, withdrawing and refusing to participate. They may daydream or become touchy or grouchy. Some may become supergood or superorganized in an attempt to put order back into their disorganized lives.

Frequent absence or tardiness. This can be caused by disorganization in the household. Children in charge of their own schedules may miss the bus or skip school. Others may be dropped off late by harried single parents who are themselves late for work.

Losing things. A child may repeatedly lose homework, a lunch box, jacket, or books, due to an inability to concentrate.

SUGGESTIONS FOR HELPING A CHILD
MAKE THE GRADE

1. Make a point of telling the child's teacher that you are in the process of divorce so that the teacher can respond to changes in the child's behavior or grades with this in mind.

2. To build self-esteem, help each child find his or her special talent or ability, and do everything you can to encourage its development. Do not demand excellence in areas where the child's talents and gifts do not lie. Instead, build up and cheer on in areas he or she does well, even if you are not personally excited by the specialty. For example, fathers who would rather see their sons become Little League stars than pianists need to work hard at developing genuine appreciation for the child's musical ability.

3. Try to keep the disorganization of the household to a minimum. Keep regular mealtimes, bedtimes, and times for rising in the morning. Designating certain hours for doing homework can promote its completion, especially if completed assignments are the tickets to privileges such as watching TV.

4. Help a forgetful child by making a checklist of things the child needs to take to school. Post this where the child will see it before going out the door in the morning.

5. For children picked up from school by different parents on different days or who take different buses depending on their daily destination, write out a note as a reminder. You might also give the teacher a copy of the note.

6. Children falling behind in schoolwork might benefit from counseling and/or private tutoring until they are able to regain their previous level of academic performance.

9
Where Is God?

How could God allow this horrible thing and say he loves me?

—Divorced mother, age thirty

How could God let this happen? It's a question both adults and children ask when divorce divides a family. It is a serious question, opening the door to other equally serious questions: Doesn't God care about what's happening to me? He's supposed to be all-powerful, so why doesn't he answer my prayers for the reconciliation of this marriage?

Jonathan has been divorced fourteen years. He recalls, "No one can imagine the disappointment a Christian has in the first impression that prayers are not answered because God doesn't really care." A little girl named Tapp remembers when her parents divorced: "I felt I was being punished by God for being really bad, so I tried being really good so God would change His mind."[1] Ten-year-old Paige, whose divorced parents are former missionaries, told me that it all boils down to this: "The parents have got to do what God wants them to do. If God wants them to get divorced, it has to be. No matter what anybody says."

Implicit in what Jonathan, Tapp, and Paige are all saying is that God could stop the divorce if he wanted to. Paige goes as far as directly attributing the divorce to God. But can this ever be the case?

The most important question to answer in this regard is whether or not God imposes his will on people. Will God force a spouse to return to a marriage that he or she wishes to leave—just because somebody prays this will happen? Does God ever cause a husband and wife to divorce or, for that matter, to remain together against their will?

Gary D. Chapman, my friend and pastor, addressed this issue in his book *Hope for the Separated*. To those who are separated but not yet divorced, he wrote,

> Your prayer must not be: "Lord, if it is Your will bring him/her back." We already know it is God's will for marriages to be restored; however, God respects human freedom . . . your spouse may choose to respond to the work of the Holy Spirit and turn from sin. On the other hand, he or she may reject all of God's pressure and walk his own way. You must give your mate the same liberty God gives.
>
> Some people blame God for allowing their marriages to break up. Do not feel that God has not answered your prayer if your spouse refuses to return. Individuals choose to get married, choose their behavior patterns toward each other, and choose to separate or resolve problems. If God did not allow such freedom He would have to reduce man to something less than man. He would have to remove the imprint of God's image in man.[2]

Said Dr. Chapman, "The truth is that God didn't send the mate away and He will not bring him or her back. God will not *make* the husband or wife return because He has given man real freedom."[3]

Both adults and children need to understand that concept. None of us are puppets. All of us are free to make choices, right or wrong, because God has given us that freedom. The Holy Spirit will influence people for righteousness in response to our prayers (John 16:8–11; Ephesians 1:18), but the decision to respond to that influence still belongs to the individual. In short, God is not to blame when marriages fail.

DAD AND GOD

James Dobson has noted, "It is a well-known fact that a child identifies his parents with God, whether or not the adults want that role."[4] It is the father in particular whom the child associates with God. We call God "Father," not "Mom" or "Grandpa." There are reasons for this: Biblically the father is the head of the family unit, as Christ is the Head of the church. The father is the final authority on what is and is not proper behavior within the home, just as the heavenly Father is the final authority on the behavior of His children. Earthly fathers work to provide food, clothing, and shelter for their families, and they do so under God's instruction and enabling. Dads provide discipline and instruction, as does our heavenly Father.

When it is the father who leaves the family, it's reasonable for children whose prayers do not seem to bring answers to wonder if God has similarly abandoned them. Children may even wonder if Dad took God with him when he left. Like it or not, parents—especially fathers—represent God in the eyes of a child.

The issue of earthly fathers representing the heavenly Father became clear to me when I met a little guy named Tommy. I was assisting in a class of first graders attending vacation Bible school at my church. Tommy and I became fast friends the first day. He was a dark-haired charmer, and I was flattered by his childish affection. He would squirm ahead of the others in line and beg to hold my hand as the class proceeded from one activity to another. He wanted my approval for his artistic accomplishments and his memorization of Bible verses. He tried to sit next to me when we went to the auditorium or the church library.

It wasn't long, however, before I realized how desperately Tommy needed my attention. If I was busy with another child or intentionally trying not to favor him over the other children, he would run to another adult for special attention. Observing this, I saw how insecure Tommy felt about himself and about almost everything he did. I began to probe my little friend gently with questions about his family. He confirmed what I had suspected:

Mom and Dad were divorced. His father lived far away in California, and Tommy missed him terribly.

One morning the class trooped into the auditorium and assembled in the choir loft for music. Tommy was in the row in front of me and several seats to my left. The music instructor began to teach the simple praise song, "Father, I Adore You." The children sang, "Father, I adore you. . . . How I love you!"

As the words soaked in, Tommy came unglued. An emotional nerve had been touched. He swung around in his seat, visibly upset. "Why are we singing this?" he sputtered. "What do they mean, *'Father,* I adore you'?"

As a teacher leaned forward and explained that the song was addressed to our *heavenly* Father, Tommy calmed considerably. As I watched, my heart ached for my little friend. Clearly, the words to the song had released his feelings for his dad.

Separating God's representatives from God is not easy for a child. The younger the child, the more Mom and Dad appear like God: omnipotent, infinitely wise, all-loving, and good. In the normal course of growing up, a child slowly realizes that parents are fallible, with frailties and faults. They make mistakes; they sin, and they fail, just as the child does.

But divorce can knock a parent from a child's pedestal almost overnight. The knowledge that parents are not all-powerful comes as a shock, and divorce may be perceived as a terrible event that no one can stop: not the child, not the parents, not even God. With no one to turn to, the child becomes disillusioned.

HIGH-RISK KIDS

Spiritually speaking, children who see no silver lining in the cloud of divorce are high-risk cases. This is especially true if their parents are professing Christians.

The serious, unspoken conclusion these kids draw from divorce is that, when put to the test, Christianity just doesn't work. And if it doesn't work, why believe?

Because the disillusionment these kids feel is so crushing, some believe that children of divorced parents who've been professing Christians are actually worse off than children from unbelieving homes. This seems true for Ricky, whose mother says he now regards his ex-pastor father as "hypocritical, untrustworthy, and selfish." Ricky's walk with the Lord appears to have come to a standstill.

In a real-life paraphrase of 1 John 4:20, children like Ricky seem to reason, *If I can't trust my parents, whom I have seen, how can I trust God, whom I have not seen?* Ironically, the *parent* has often taught the child the very values and morality that the parent's lifestyle now contradicts.

SORTING IT OUT

Divorce may pose a child's stiffest spiritual challenge. Tim LaHaye has said,

> The most mixed-up children do not come from excessively strict homes, but those where teaching and example live in conflict. . . . What turns young people against Christ and His church is to hear the parents give lip service to Bible standards of morality but practice the reverse in the home.[5]

When it comes to parental modeling the proverbial expression is true: Actions speak louder than words. A child will usually internalize the parent's behavior before internalizing any verbal assertions about right and wrong. When actions and words contradict each other, the child must struggle to sort truth from error.

Twenty-seven-year-old Brandon is concerned for his children, knowing they will eventually have to sort out what has happened. "Later on in their lives they'll look back on the fact that we broke up and that the Bible says it's wrong. I think they'll have trouble with that: *If this is wrong, why did you do it?* I think it's definitely going to stay with them for the rest of their lives."

Other single parents live with the burden of seeing how divorce has affected their children's spiritual lives. Glenn, age thirty, was not awarded custody of his daughters, ages eight and eleven. He said, "I think my children are not getting as good a training as they would have under my care. Spiritually my children are zero. No one can imagine the heartache I have for my children's lives.''

Others, like Kathy, are optimistic: "Spiritually, my child is not lacking. God has given me grace to persevere and purpose to lead her spiritually.'' Sandy believes her children have been spiritually strengthened by her divorce. "I think they will be real lights in the world because of what they've been through.''

TWO RESPONSES

Divorce can draw some children closer to God. Kimberlee, a seventh grader, said, "I think divorce is something that teaches faith. I am a Christian and I praise God no matter what.''

Other children become so disillusioned by their parents' behavior that they turn away from God. When the minister-father of fourteen-year-old Ricky became involved with another woman and divorced his wife, Ricky's response, according to his sister, was to shut God out of his life. "I think he was mad at God,'' she said. "I think he didn't understand how God could allow this to happen. I think he still is mad because he complains about having to go to church and all this, and he won't pray anymore—even just at the dinner table, saying grace.''

Children who live in the emotional war zone of a divorcing household are not much different from those who reside in military war zones when it comes to their perception of God's hand in their circumstances. *Time* magazine visited and interviewed children in five war zones around the world and found that no matter what kind of tragedy befell their families, some responded by blaming God while others wisely discerned where the blame really belongs.

Elizabeth, a sixteen-year-old Irish girl whose mother, brother, and grandfather had all been killed in the ongoing violence between Protestants and Catholics in Belfast, told her interviewer, "When we were younger we couldn't understand it. We didn't know where to turn or who to blame. We asked adults, and the adults, they all had different views of it. I kept askin', 'Why is all this happenin' to *us?*' '' Her interviewer responded,

"Did it shake your belief in God?" Elizabeth replied, "Not in God. In man."

Following a devastating explosion, Ahmed, a fifteen-year-old Palestinian boy, was asked, "Do you think: How could God allow such a thing to happen?" Ahmed answered, "No. There is no relationship between God and the people who do such things. Man does his work, God his."

But an Israeli girl named Hadara felt different about the tragedy surrounding her. After the terrorist killing of an entire family whose children she baby-sat, Hadara was devastated and cynical. She wrote:

> If there's a God
> and yes, many claim there is,
> then how does it happen
> that little kids get killed?[6]

Whether there is verbal crossfire within the walls of one's own home, or a real exchange of bullets and bombs within the borders of one's city, there will always be children who interpret it the way Kimberlee, Elizabeth, and Ahmed do. And there will always be those who doubt and blame God, as Ricky and Hadara do.

Most of the children with whom I talked while writing this book felt that divorce had actually drawn them closer to God and to the family members they lived with. These were typical comments:

God loves me very much.

I wasn't mad at God. That was where I went to. I guess you could say I ran to him.

God knows all, so he's my only true friend.

It's a comfort to say a prayer at night to God. He's really one person who listens to me and helps take the burden away.

Divorce is rough, and most kids turn to drugs; not me, I turn to God.

I believe that any child who turns to God in the face of parental divorce will be much better off than one who does not—even if that turning is just the barest starting point of a relationship with God. In Christ there is hope and a source of help and healing that transcends the best human efforts to comfort a child of divorce.

Consider Anita, who was twelve when her parents divorced. According to her brother,

> Six months before the separation that caught us all off guard, Anita had recurring dreams that her parents were divorced. She believes that it was God, reaching out to her, strengthening her, helping her become familiar with unknown and painful territory. Healing was taking place before any of us were conscious of the wounds. That is a testimony both to God's grace and to Anita's deep sensitivity to others and to God.[7]

I asked Kimberlee about her experience as a Christian child of divorce. She told me, "When I got old enough to understand what Christianity was, I prayed about everything that I didn't understand, and most of the time God gave me an answer to every question I had. Most of the time he did."

"That's neat," I remarked.

"It sure is," Kim said with a smile. "It's a *relief!*"

SUGGESTIONS FOR HELPING A CHILD SPIRITUALLY

1. Help children understand that parents, not God, willed the divorce to happen. They may find comfort in hearing that God would like the relationship to be reconciled as much as they would, but that God lets everyone—parents and boys and girls—make choices. If parents choose to divorce, God will not stop them even though divorce makes him sad.

2. Encourage children to tell God all their feelings, fears, and anxieties. Pray with and for them about each of their concerns.

3. Parents can enhance their own relationships with God by becoming active in a Bible-believing church that welcomes single-parent families. Most pastors would be happy to answer questions about their church fellowship or about establishing a personal relationship with God through Christ. Don't give up the search for a church home until you find a place where both parent and child can be spiritually nourished

and emotionally encouraged. (See the Appendix if you are unsure how to establish a personal relationship with God.)

4. Make up a promise box of encouraging Bible verses from a modern version such as the *New International Version*. Write verses on separate slips of paper, fold them, and place them in a box or coffee can. Allow the child to draw out one promise to claim each day, perhaps during breakfast. Discuss the meaning of the verse and how it applies to the child's life. Here are some verses you might want to include.

John 14:27	James 4:8a	Proverbs 16:20
Romans 8:28	Romans 5:3–4	Proverbs 1:33
James 1:2–4	Philippians 4:6–7	Hebrews 13:5
Isaiah 26:3	1 Peter 5:7	Psalm 34:19
Psalm 18:32	Isaiah 55:8–9	Luke 12:7

5. Involve the child in Sunday school, vacation Bible school, church camp, or other church-related activities designed for children.

6. Parents can make a practice of holding family worship times. Keep these short enough to hold a child's attention. Include some form of prayer and Bible reading. With very young children, prayers can be mere sentences and Bible reading can be a few verses or from a Bible storybook. Singing, holding hands, and acting out stories can make this a warm, enjoyable time for both parent and child.

7. Make a prayer-request journal. On the lefthand pages of a notebook list petitions you and the child are making to God. On the opposite pages record how and when God answers.

8. Keep in mind that children identify parents with God. Give love and approval *unconditionally*. Don't allow the child to feel that if his or her grades were better or if he had made the team or if she were better looking or if he were a she you would love the child more. Let each child know that he or she is a unique, special, and precious person to you.

10
Money Matters

People at church don't understand what it's like to be poor. If rich people knew what it was like, they would like me.

—Kimberlee, age twelve

Divorce introduces financial and material changes into a child's lifestyle. And the financial hardship that often accompanies divorce is a major cause for lowered self-esteem. Children who always viewed themselves as well off or middle class may suddenly see themselves as poor. Even when basic needs for food, clothing, and shelter are met, they may feel impoverished compared with the way life used to be, or compared with their peers. Self-esteem is lowered because of the cultural weight put on possessions and economic strength. "The hardest part about having divorced parents," said one thirteen-year-old girl, "is facing rich friends."

Many children of divorce in long-term tight-money situations must routinely forfeit opportunities for personal growth and enrichment. Tickets to a concert, a play, or a sporting event are rare. Lessons of any sort, whether ballet, piano, gymnastics, or tennis, can be afforded only with extraordinary sacrifice. Similarly, cosmetic luxuries such as orthodontic braces or contact lenses rather than eyeglasses may be low financial priorities. Purchasing clothes in the current fashions may be out of the question. Little or no spending money may be available for recreational activities with friends at the movies or community pool.

All these restraints affect a child's self-image in relationship to peers. Boys may be more sensitive than girls to the effects of family economic woes. Interviewers for the Children of Divorce Project detected "a significant link between depression in younger boys and the reduced social and economic circumstances in the postdivorce family."[1]

THE FEMINIZATION OF POVERTY

Divorce is largely responsible for what is now being called "the feminization of poverty." In many instances divorce splits the family into two economic camps: men who fare well and custodial mothers who are impoverished. In the wake of divorce, these women and children find themselves struggling with what sociologist Susan Anderson-Khlief has called a "strong sense of downward mobility."[2] A majority of single parent families (sixty-two percent) have incomes below $20,000 a year.[3]

The family home may have been sold, forcing family members into smaller dwellings, sometimes in housing or neighborhoods previously considered unacceptable. A mother who has not worked outside the home before the divorce may suddenly find herself in the job market, unable to obtain anything but low paying, low status work. Child-support payments and other financial help from the noncustodial parent may be inconsistent, minimal, or nonexistent. According to information provided by the Office of Child Support Enforcement, "Only about 60% of mothers heading a single parent family have a child support award, and of these women, only 48% receive the full amount due and 26% receive nothing."[4] Even those who receive the full amount often find it woefully inadequate and unrealistic compared to what it really costs to raise a child.

Sometimes the period of economic chaos is only temporary. If adequate child-support arrangements can be agreed upon and if the custodial parent already has or is soon able to find a good job, the family's financial state may soon approximate the predivorce conditions. Affluent families may experience only minimal financial adjustment after divorce.

But most often, there is no question that, at least financially, women and children are the losers in divorce. Single mother families are five times more likely than two-parent families to be living below the poverty line.[5] One researcher found that, on average, a woman with children experiences a 73 percent decline in income after divorce. However, "most social scientists now believe that a 30% drop may be nearer the truth; bad—but less disastrous."[6] Whatever the decline, it contributes to the feeling that "something terrible has happened to us." A great many single-mother families are now poor in their own eyes, and they may feel tremendously embarrassed about it.

Sandy, a thirty-seven-year-old mother, typifies the single mother hardest hit by divorce. Her income, earned as a typist for an insurance company, combined with the child support she receives from her former husband, provides barely enough for her to raise her three children.

Sandy and her children believe that the key to their economic survival has been their faith in Christ and in his purposes for their lives. Their financial difficulties are pervasive and ongoing, yet they cope remarkably well with little, very much aware, Sandy says, "of how God takes care of us." She spoke candidly when I interviewed her.

> We have suffered, and we still are suffering terribly, financially. I am very frank with the kids. I tell them, "You see this bill right here? I can't pay this. There's not enough money. I gave the landlord a check for the rent, but there's not enough money in the bank. And my car insurance is due in three days!" And they know that, and we pray about it. The kids have seen how God provides for us; those kids' faith is as deep as mine.
>
> Because of our economic situation, I do not buy clothes. The clothes that we wear are given to us, and we take what we get. It's been hard, especially for the girls, as far as the peer attitude. My older daughter is getting to be a teenager and she is more clothes conscious. I can't just go out and buy the latest fashions. It's hard in a single-parent situation. Most of the kids my children run around with have both parents and lots of money, everything they need. And here's my daughter with her meager clothes.

I'm not saying I don't take help, because there are times when people help us along the way and I couldn't make it without them.

The children have had some opportunities to do some things that are high on my priority list as far as how the money is spent, not only for their basic needs but for their emotional needs. I forked out eighty-five dollars in the middle of December so my son could go on a trip with the youth group, and I didn't have it. I still don't. But to me that eighty-five dollars was important. There are a lot of things I do for them that I don't really have the money for, because they have to be well-balanced emotionally.

There's nothing worse than a kid who grows up and says, "Well, my parents were divorced when I was little, and we never got to go anywhere or do anything." And they're miserable and unhappy because they had a miserable childhood. When my kids grow up, they're going to remember poverty, but they're going to remember a good, happy, fulfilled childhood. Sometimes people do not understand my priorities, but I'm the one raising those kids, and I have peace with God that I've done the right thing.

MOM'S ATTITUDE IS THE KEY

Custodial mothers often feel angry about the inequities they see when they compare their circumstances with those of their ex-husbands. While the women struggle to make ends meet, men typically experience a forty-two percent *rise* in their standard of living in the first year after divorce.[7] In addition, many remember the higher standard of living the whole family shared before the divorce. Both mothers and children may struggle with feelings of deprivation, anger toward the father, and a sense that life is grossly unfair.

The most important factor in a child's adjustment to reduced income after divorce may well be the mother's attitude. The way she feels about her financial circumstances—and her ex-husband—has a significant impact on the way her children will cope with their economic circumstances and respond to their father.

Henry Biller noted, "The mother's attitudes are related to her social and economic opportunities and are readily transmitted to the child."[8] Children of Divorce Project researchers found similarly, "The children's response to the economic pressures in the family was mediated through the mother-child relationship. Their adjustment was not directly affected by the economic circumstances alone."[9]

CAN MONEY TALK?

The typical financial advantage of fathers over mothers after divorce can be particularly destructive when used to sway a child's loyalties. In such cases the child is tempted materially and forced to choose between a "have" and a "have-not" parent. The real issue here, of course, is that the child is used as a pawn in the ongoing parental dispute.

Brenda, a forty-four-year-old divorced mother, is familiar with the problem. Her son Paul, twelve, lives with his father. Paul seems caught in the struggle between the "have" and the "have-not" parent. Brenda, the "have-not" parent, has anxiously watched her son turn first one way and then the other. When Brenda and I first talked, she was pursuing custody of Paul.

> I feel he would be in a better environment should he be with me, even though . . . my ex-husband can buy Paul everything he wants.
>
> I told Paul, "If you come to live with me, I cannot give you all these material things. The only thing I can give you is love and understanding." He's very torn. He said, "If I go with you, Mom, Dad will be mad. If I go with Dad, you'll be mad." And I told him, "Paul that's not so. I will always love you." I really don't feel that he has that assurance from his dad.

Karen, a twelve-year-old from a midsized southern city, has the reverse of Paul's problem. The "have-not" parent, her mother, is the one applying the manipulative pressure. Karen's father has had very little contact with her for several years and that hurts her very much. Yet Karen's mother has told her clearly what to expect if Karen should ever be swayed by her father's financial advantage. Karen explained,

> See, my father is rich now. He could offer me anything. He could buy me a car right now. My mom said, "I don't care what he

offers you. If he offers you three or four cars when you grow up, don't accept. And don't go with him. If you do, I could probably never forgive you, because I've stayed with you this whole time."

Kids like Paul and Karen have been placed in a difficult and uncomfortable position by their parents. The desire to know and relate in a positive way to both parents is a normal, God-given desire. When money is used as a weapon in the ongoing parental war, the best interests of the child are laid aside. Whether money is an issue or not, any time a parent demands that a child renounce a relationship with the other parent, that child is likely to become depressed, anxious, and preoccupied with the unresolved dilemma. Many feel caught in the middle. Seventeen-year-old Anna lamented, "My mother needs to understand that I need to have a relationship with my dad. I need him in my life right now."

Research has shown that the children who cope best with divorce are those who maintain stable, close relationships with both their custodial and their noncustodial parents. In other words, kids need good relationships with both parents to make the best adjustment after divorce. A parent who attempts to buy a child's loyalty or threatens to withdraw love if the child sells out to the other parent diminishes the chances for the child's good recovery.

POOR BABIES

A more benevolent version of the "money talks" idea is "poor babies," a term referring to adults' attempts to compensate children materially for the unhappiness divorce brings into their lives. Anyone can participate—parents, grandparents, aunts and uncles, boyfriends and girlfriends of the parents, and anybody else who can be made to feel sorry for the children.

To a point, extra compensation is a good idea. Children of divorce need reassurance that they are loved and cared about. To some children a gift from an adult says "I love you" more clearly than anything else. Sometimes a gift or a special outing or treat can help to ward off insecurity or loneliness that may be cropping up. A multitude of genuine practical needs can be met legitimately by others without overdoing it: school clothes, haircuts, lunch money, or tuition, for example.

The poor-babies attitude does not become a problem until adults express love in this way too often. When child survivors of a divorce war are routinely indulged with an inordinate amount of goods, they quickly join the ranks of those our grandparents would have considered spoiled. Showered with gifts, toys, money, and treats from gullible adults, these children are quick to learn that with little effort they can obtain almost anything they want. A little pouting or crying goes a long way: Someone always comes through with the desired item. "After all, his parents are divorced, poor baby."

These pampered children can easily grow up with a distorted perception of love. They may subscribe to the notion that they should be catered to in a similar fashion by teachers, employers, and future spouses—not exactly a prescription for success!

Only a portion of the children of divorce experience this kind of treatment, of course, but they can be found in almost any postdivorce setting, whether affluent or financially struggling. (The economic posture of those outside the single-parent family—usually generous relatives—makes it possible.) Certainly much depends on the children themselves. Those already bent toward greed, deprivation, or manipulation are prime "poor babies" candidates.

David Martin, a Christian counselor, told me,

> What I've seen most in the children that I've counseled is that all of a sudden they start getting a whole lot more gifts. Grandparents start supplying them with things that they could never have had when they were with the parents. Boyfriends or girlfriends of the parent bring them gifts to try to win their affection, and they become spoiled. This is especially the case with single children. They become spoiled to the point where they expect gifts. And if the parent marries this boyfriend or girlfriend and the gifts stop coming, that's usually when I start seeing the children.

Noncustodial fathers are often the greatest indulgers. Even in intact families, the father is traditionally the parent "from whom all blessings flow," as Biller and Meredith put it in their book *Father Power*. They noted,

> The father may . . . give gifts to his children to gain a feeling of control, of adequacy, or of being needed in the family. He may feel that he is an outsider, a walking wallet. Thus, he may use the only power he feels he has, the power of money, to ingratiate himself into his child's life.[10]

If this is true of fathers who are still married to the mothers of their children, it can be more sadly true for fathers who are separated from their children after divorce. Divorced fathers may feel even more compelled to play Santa Claus in an attempt to appease their consciences regarding the divorce or to make up for a lack of time spent with their children. In the Wallerstein sampling, "at least one-third of the men were unusually generous to their children, plying them with special treats or money. . . . This role strained the fathers financially and emotionally and . . . often angered their divorcing wives."[11]

Mothers and stepmothers can be guilty of playing Santa, too. In fact, when both sides of the family are "haves," the whole poor-babies issue gets even stickier. Children, of course, enjoy material things and will seldom refuse adult generosity. But no amount of material gratification will ever provide more than a superficial nurture for a child, whose greatest needs are more emotional than material. Even the most extravagant gifts will do little to make a child feel more secure or less afraid after divorce. Children need a competent, involved parent far more than they need anything a parent could purchase for them.

"Attempts at bribery do not escape the child," write Biller and Meredith. "He knows when he is being bought, when material things are being used in place of true nurturance."[12]

CHILD SUPPORT ISSUES

Many fathers might like to play Santa but cannot. They can barely pay their own bills, let alone meet their legal child-support obligations. Others, for a variety of reasons, deliberately withhold not only child support, but also support of any kind, including gifts, vacations, and clothes. In fact, one out of five fathers, according to research, has never provided any type of assistance.[13]

Middle- and upper-income fathers tend to be more regular in child-support payments and in visitation than men in the lower brackets. These two issues—child support and visitation—appear to be separate aspects of fathering after divorce, and they are treated that way by the legal system, but in reality they are closely linked.

Research has shown that whether or not child support is paid may hinge on the relationship between the former spouses more than on the father's income level.[14] Men who can afford to make child-support payments sometimes deliberately withhold them as a protest when former wives refuse to allow them child visitation.

That doesn't discount the fact that some men let child support slide when they must choose between paying their rent and making child-support payments. Payments may be sporadic at best. Their financial liability makes them feel sheepish about visiting and ensures that their former wives are less happy to have them do so. In this case the children lose twice. They miss out on much-needed time with their fathers, and they miss out on much-needed financial support. For the well-being of the father-child relationship, this kind of impasse should be resolved quickly.

Women find it easier to take legal recourse regarding child support than men do regarding visitation. The reason for this, according to family law attorney Christine Gale, is that "child support is not considered the mother's right. It's the child's right." She told me, "Even if the mother absolutely refuses to let the father see the child, the father can be brought into court to pay child support, and if he doesn't comply they can get a wage attachment and it'll be taken right out of his pay."

Fathers face a much tougher battle if they wish to see their kids when the mothers are against it. Often it means repeated court appearances, legal fees, and lots of hassle, especially if mother and child reside in a different city or state, since the litigation usually takes place where they live. Only rarely are fathers willing to go through the long procedure that may be necessary to obtain their rights. It doesn't happen very often, says Gale, "unless the father *really* wants to see those kids and doesn't care about the time that he spends or the inconvenience."

Gale notes that mothers who feel stronger about the fathers' not seeing the children than they do about receiving child support may be saying in effect, " 'If you just drop everything about visitation I won't sue you for child support' and it's kind of a silent agreement that neither one of them is going to pursue their legal rights and obligations."

By contrast, mothers who really want the father to visit are sometimes frustrated by the resistance they meet. Christine Gale says,

> There are a lot of cases that I've had where the father doesn't care about visitation and doesn't pursue it and just wants out altogether. When the divorce takes place he divorces the kids just as much as the parent. So visitation is something the mother can't force the father to do. It's the father's right, but it's not considered the father's legal obligation. You can get a court order forcing the father to pay support, but you can't get a court order forcing the father to visit the child. . . . It would be a little bit difficult to force the father to visit the child—how would you go about it? You can't force a parent to care; you *can* force a parent to pay.

MAKING THE MOST OF WHAT YOU HAVE

Many custodial parents wisely recognize that meeting their children's emotional and social needs is as important as meeting material needs. Sandy, quoted earlier, is a good example: "There are a lot of things I do for them that I don't really have the money for, because they have to be well-balanced emotionally."

One positive by-product of economic hardship can be an enhanced appreciation for both the parent and the things in life that don't come with a price tag. Paige told me, "I don't have a lot of clothes, but I have toys and stuff. But my mom gives to us more than she gives to herself." Kimberlee said, "When people try to show their love, they spend time with children, just doing things with them. They don't have to spend money—just take them to the park, cook them lunch, or do anything that makes them feel good, feel loved.''

SUGGESTIONS FOR HELPING CHILDREN ADJUST TO NEW FINANCIAL SITUATIONS

1. Emphasize character qualities rather than possessions or appearance. Memorizing and discussing Proverbs is an excellent way to accomplish this.
2. Since the mother's attitude is a key factor in the child's development, moms will want to work at maintaining a positive outlook. Supportive friendships and practical matters such as learning to budget are important. Counseling with a pastor or therapist may be helpful to a woman struggling with bitterness, resentment, or envy toward a more prosperous ex-husband.

PART FOUR

FAMILY TIES

11

The Grandparent Connection

What most people don't understand about divorce is that it doesn't just affect children and parents, but grandparents, friends, neighbors, relatives. . . .

—Bob, age sixteen

Children enjoy a unique kind of relationship with grandparents. Here there is an immunity of sorts; children do not have to please or perform in quite the same way that they do for their parents. And grandparents can claim the status of being seasoned child-care experts—with the added pleasure of not having to take full responsibility. They can enjoy their grandchildren and then return them to the parents in time to prevent an overdose.

The grandparent-grandchild relationship is often a mutually beneficial, warm, and positive experience. Youngsters benefit from Grandma and Grandpa's wisdom and experience; grandparents thrive on the spontaneity, love, and companionship of their children's children. Many an older person has found renewed purpose for living because of grandchildren; in return, many grandparents are able to provide children with a special boost to their self-esteem.

SEVERED ROOTS

Because of our increased mobility, our society as a whole is losing its sense of extended family. This may be a contributing factor in many divorces. For example, only 10 percent of the divorcing families observed in the Children of Divorce Project had any extended family geographically nearby. Most couples were isolated nuclear families struggling with their problems without the support of sisters, brothers, parents, or in-laws close enough to sit and chat over a cup of coffee.

But even long-distance grandparent-grandchild relationships can be cherished and fulfilling, with phone calls, cards, photographs, and letters filling in the gaps between visits.

Whether they live across town or across the country, many grandparents have known the heartbreak of suddenly being labeled "off-limits" due to divorce. One of the most unfortunate by-products of divorce is the way it can interfere with the grandchild-grandparent relationship. The two generations that had nothing to do with the couple's breakup are divorced from one another, often under great protest from both. Half a child's extended family may be "lost" to the child, uprooting his or her support system and sense of identity.

Divorce can muddle a child's sense of identity. To illustrate, let's consider a hypothetical little girl named Molly Jones. Let's say that Molly's parents get divorced. Her mother then marries John Stone. Molly would still be Molly Jones even though her mother is now Mrs. Stone, but Mr. Stone adopts Molly, so she becomes Molly Stone. Let's assume that Molly's mother and Mr. Stone then get a divorce. Molly's mother gets custody of Molly and goes into a third marriage to Mr. Jeffries. Mr. Jeffries does not adopt Molly. If this marriage lasts and Mr. and Mrs. Jeffries have children, Molly will have a different last name than everyone else in her family, a name that belongs to someone not even biologically related to her.

Look at the adjustments Molly will have made. First, she will have had in essence three fathers: her biological father, her adopted father, and her new stepfather. She will have had to adjust her identity three times, first being Molly Jones, then Molly Stone, and finally an outsider named Stone in a family named Jeffries. And Molly could be claimed as a grandchild by at least four sets of grandparents, both biological and "adopted."

When family roots are dug up and scattered, children are the biggest losers. They lose a sense of their heritage. When they lose touch with a grandparent, they lose another mirror on their lives and often one of the friendliest ones. They also lose a relationship that could have been a significant source of comfort and perspective on the divorce itself.

Custodial mothers are are often responsible for closing the door on a grandparent-grandchild relationship. According to family law attorney Christine Gale, this is most likely to happen when the father has died. She said, "The mother may use his death to sever contact between the paternal grandparents and the children." More commonly, paternal grandparents and their grandchildren lose touch because the children's father is "out of the picture" and not taking responsibility for arranging visits between his children and parents.

GRANDPARENT VISITATION

Not all grandparents wish to be highly involved in the lives of their grandchildren. In their observations of sixty families in the process of divorce, Wallerstein and Kelly found that only half of the maternal grandparents and less than half the paternal grandparents maintained regular contact with their grandchildren.

But many grandparents are unwilling to stand passively by when their relationships are severed. An increasing number are willing to go to court to obtain the right to visit their grandchildren. Though statutes vary from state to state, all states now give grandparents the legal right to go to court. Even so, those who pursue this option may have to invest considerable time and money with no real guarantee as to the outcome; if awarded visitation rights, grandparents still may not get to see the children as much as they would like. If the custodial parent moves out of the state in which the suit was brought, visitation becomes difficult, requiring changes in the court order. "Any custody order," said Christine Gale, "has to be practical. If the distance is great, then the grandparents would have to bear the expense of transportation and would have to accommodate more to the children's needs."

Gale feels that if maintaining a relationship with grandparents was determined to be in the child's best interests, "the court would go out of its way to come up with an order where the grandparents would be able to visit."

Determining the best interests of a child can involve many factors, including the age of the child, the degree of emotional closeness between the child and grandparents, the degree of interest shown by the grandparents, and how active they have been in the child's life in years past. One key element is the kind of relationship that currently exists between the custodial parent and the grandparents. "If the custodial parent absolutely despises the grandparents and mere contact is going to cause a lot of tension and a lot of aggravation, the court might determine that it's just not in the best interests of the children to have that tension continue," Gale said.

Grandparents who are determined to win the right to visit with their grandchildren should be prepared to answer the common defenses against this arrangement: inconvenience because of distance or a lack of involvement in the lives of the children before the divorce occurred.

Many legal professionals and mental health experts now agree, however, that the best interests of the child usually include the right to a relationship with both sets of grandparents. The social and emotional fulfillment that grandparents and grandchildren bring to each other should be allowed to continue after divorce.

PROVIDING LOVE AND SUPPORT

While grandparents' love and encouragement may not be able to make up for the problems at home, many grandchildren have been tremendously lifted—even if only temporarily—by the respite provided by Grandma and Grandpa. Judith Wallerstein has written,

Grandparents can play a particular role, especially if their marriages are intact: symbolic generational continuity and living proof to children that relationships can be lasting, reliable, and dependable. Grandparents also convey a sense of tradition and a special commitment to the young. . . . Their encouragement, friendship, and affection has special meaning for children of divorce; it specifically counteracts the children's sense that all relationships are unhappy and transient."[1]

Psychologist Archibald Hart has recalled,

My grandparents were extremely loving and supportive to my brother and me during this period of divorce. If they were angry at my parents, they never showed or talked about it to us. They never interfered, except to invite us to visit them as often as we wanted. We slipped in a few weekend visits that were not a part of our regular visiting schedule, and those visits were like oases in the desert. They provided relief from the tensions at home and helped me to keep my perspective.[2]

Several single-parent families with whom I spoke named grandparents on both sides of the family as primary supports. Brett and his two sisters would go home to an empty house after school if it weren't for their maternal grandmother, who keeps them until their mother comes home from work. Brett's mother said, "I have the real support of both sides—my ex-husband's and mine. I'm closer to his parents than he is, because they totally support me and the kids and they do not condone at all what he's done. His mother and I are more like mother and daughter."

Statistics reveal that almost three million children under the age of eighteen reside with their grandparents. In most cases, three generations live together under one roof, with one or both parents also present. But at least 882,000 kids are being raised solely by their grandparents, with neither parent in the picture.[3] This is a 16 percent increase compared with figures from a decade ago, reflecting not only divorce, but also other social ills such as drug abuse, teen pregnancy, and economic hardships.[4]

To Jack, age ten, and his sister, Carla, twelve, Grandmother is a very special person, in many ways the only mother they have ever known. Jack, Carla, and their father, Steve, have lived with Steve's mother in her Arkansas home since the children were toddlers. And Grandma, not Dad, has legal custody of the children. Steve explained that there were two reasons for this: "So we could get them on her insurance plan, so they would be covered medically at a reasonable amount." And to allow Steve to pursue his undergraduate degree and then seminary. Steve said, "My wife and I were not in the best kind of financial situation, which was one of the problems in our marriage. So when we split up I could not afford to rent a place of my own. My mother said that we could move in with her, so I did that. And she helped just tremendously."

Many grandparents have felt somewhat hemmed in when a son or daughter's divorce has essentially brought them a second family to raise. Leola Archer was a bit reluctant at first to assume this role. When her son and his two children, ages two and five, temporarily moved back home after his divorce, she had to limit her activities to meet the needs of her expanded family. Five years later, when a grandson, Jimmy, came to live with her permanently, she had to make major changes in her schedule and lifestyle.

"Ten years had passed and I was still in limbo," she wrote. Then one day while at the kitchen sink, she felt Jimmy's arm encircle her waist. With his mouth full of food, he whispered in her ear, "Grandma, you're just like Jesus." Sensing that his grandmother was puzzled, he continued, "I was a stranger and you took me in, naked and you clothed me, sick and you visited me, hungry and you gave me food. Isn't that like Jesus?"

With that Jimmy walked away and left the room. But at the door he turned around and said, "You know something else? I believe you were put here special—special just for me."[5]

SUGGESTIONS FOR GRANDPARENTS

1. If you are aware of marital difficulties in your child's home, invite your grandchildren to spend escape time with you. This might mean their spending a weekend every so often or maybe your taking them out for dinner, to the park, or someplace special whenever possible.

2. Be a good listener. If the child is willing to share feelings and frustrations about what is happening at home, let him or her know that you will keep the conversation in confidence. Do not scold for or attempt to correct feelings. Be a friend, not a critic.

3. Be careful not to voice criticisms about the divorce or either parent and avoid the temptation to take sides in any way when the grandchildren are present.

4. Long-distance grandparenting is worth the trouble. Letters, phone calls, photos, and other forms of communication help assure children that they have roots and that their grandparents care about them. Grandparents who can afford it may want to give grandchildren permission to call collect when they really need to talk. This could be a great comfort for some during divorce.

SUGGESTION FOR PARENTS

When the natural grandparent-grandchild relationship has been severed or when grandparents live far away, you might invite older neighbors or church friends into your home. In this way children can receive some of the blessings and benefits of interacting with older people. Perhaps they will want to adopt substitute grandparents. Older folks might seek to adopt some children who need grandparents by developing a special friendship with them.

12
Solo Parenting

*It's not really fun not having two parents. Some-
times it's a lot of hassle.*

—Paige, age ten

In the early part of this century, fathers had the absolute
right of custody after divorce. In society's view the father was
better equipped than the mother to provide for the children
financially and educationally. In the rare event that custody was
awarded to the mother, the father then had no further legal
responsibility to provide for the child.

By the 1920s the pendulum had swung in the other
direction. Motherhood was so elevated in the popular consciousness that maternal rather than paternal custody became
the rule and eventually the law.[1]

Today, society's concern for equality of the sexes has
opened the door once again to father custody, even though
mothers are still given custody nine times out of ten. Fathers
who challenge a custody decision, however, stand a good chance
of winning.

According to 1990 census figures, there are 9.7 million
single-parent families in this country. Of these, 8.4 million are
headed by single mothers and 1.3 million by single fathers.
Single-parent families are three times more common among
blacks than among whites.

WOE IS ONE

By divine design, parenting is a task for two. This is especially evident in the life of Jesus. Since Christ was born of a virgin, in a technical sense God didn't "need" Joseph. Yet God knew that Mary needed a husband, especially in the culture of her times. She needed physical and emotional support and help during and after the long journey to Bethlehem where the baby was born.

By God's design Mary was given a partner to coparent the only sinless child ever born. And by God's design the very Son of God was given two earthly parents who would help prepare him for his mission to humanity. If this family is an example for the rest of us, the message is clear: Parenting is a job big enough and important enough to require the combined strength and energy of two people.

When two people combine their efforts to accomplish something greater than either of them could have achieved alone, this is called *synergism*. To a large degree, it is the positive synergism of the marriage relationship that enables a man and woman together to accomplish the task of parenting. Ecclesiastes 4:9–12 is a good illustration of synergism.

> *Two are better than one,*
> *because they have a good return for their work:*
> *If one falls down,*
> *his friend can help him up.*
> *But pity the man who falls*
> *and has no one to help him up!*
> *Also, if two lie down together, they will keep warm.*
> *But how can one keep warm alone?*
> *Though one may be overpowered,*
> *two can defend themselves.*

When a marriage weakens and dies, synergism ceases between the parents. Often one parent is left with a major portion of the responsibilities and little or no further help or support from the former spouse. He or she must assume the difficult task of parenting solo.

Brandon, a twenty-seven-year-old single father, expressed it like this:

I realize that by choosing to keep the kids in my custody it is an awful lot of work, an awful lot more responsibility than I had before. It's not shared any longer; it's all mine. When you're the only one doing it, you have to go to work all day and come home and work all night. You finally get to sit down around ten o'clock at night and unwind. It's not that terrible, don't take it wrong. It's just that by the time you make supper and clean up, it's seven or eight o'clock; then you've got to get the kids ready for bed and read them a story. You don't even have that much time to spend with them, the time you'd like to have. Then when they're in bed you've got more to do: keeping after the house, keeping the wash caught up, keeping the bills paid. There's so much.

Kathy, thirty-three, framed her situation with these words:

Once you're used to functioning as two people in two roles and all of a sudden you're one person but still two roles—how do you handle it? I struggle with having to work all day, having to pay for everything, having to do everything in the house, take care of the car, pay medical bills, do all the shopping, try to have a social life, try to find baby-sitters, and then feel guilty because I don't see Katie as often as I want to! The point is, there's never enough time or energy to be Mom and Dad both and it's very difficult not to feel guilty.

The stress both Kathy and Brandon feel seems to stem from trying, as Kathy said, "to be Mom and Dad both." It is a frustrating role!

In trying to fulfill the roles of both mother and father, these single parents are in a sense seeking to be androgynous—both male and female at the same time. Because of their love for their children and their sense of responsibility, they have succeeded to a measurable degree. But while God created some androgynous members of the plant kingdom, he did not create any androgynous people.

No woman, no matter how firmly and consistently she disciplines or how successful she may be in the workplace, can ever communicate to a child what it means to be masculine. No man, no matter how warm or gentle or how emotionally supportive he may be, can ever adequately demonstrate to a son or daughter what it means to be feminine.

As they attempt to fill the role of their missing partner,

single fathers and single mothers each encounter a different set of problems.

THE CASE OF THE MISSING FATHER

Discipline

Women who parent without a partner commonly struggle in the area of child discipline. Hetherington, Cox, and Cox found that children—especially boys—tend to behave more poorly with mothers than with fathers. Their research showed that during the difficult first year after divorce, especially, children in single mother families were "more dependent, disobedient, aggressive, whining, demanding and unaffectionate than children in intact families."[2]

During this time, the mother is under more emotional stress than previously, is busier, and is less apt to be patient. Her focus in child discipline may be simply to make her children comply with her requests instead of to develop the child's character. She may be less affectionate following discipline and less inclined to provide verbal explanations about the child's offense.

Mothers tend to be more affectionate toward daughters than toward sons at this time, perhaps because they are directing resentment for the father toward their sons. At any rate, mothers tend to expect better behavior and more independence from their sons, while giving them less support than they give to their daughters. A recent study found that "boys are more likely than girls to have difficult relationships with their mothers, and the negative mother-son relationship contributes to the emotional difficulties of boys."[3]

When boys sense that Mom's support is lacking, they respond by becoming more demanding, fearful, argumentative, and resentful. This touches off a mother-son conflict that can be serious and long-running. Ben, who is ten, told me, "My mother seems terrible and mean because we are around each other so much. I wish my mother would work on her temper."

But even when a mother has no sons, discipline can still be hard. Mary Beth, who is eight, complained, "My mother is always in a bad mood and spanks me." Fifteen-year-old Sarah has noticed her mother's difficulties. She said, "I think she has more trouble being the disciplinarian, showing authority over us, and she's having to take on a lot of the role that my dad used to have. And it's still hard on her; I can see it. It stresses her so much that after she has to do something to either one of us she'll just go into her bedroom and cry."

What's missing from the home after divorce is the father's authority. One study showed that even if fathers said and did *nothing,* their mere presence in the home was enough to make a child more likely to comply with the mother's requests for discipline.

Time with Dad

To some extent every single parent must mediate the relationship between the absent parent and the children.

A recent nationwide survey of 1,423 children revealed that 23 percent of their fathers had not been in contact with them during the previous five years. An additional 20 percent had not seen their children during the previous year.[4] Another nationwide study indicates than 40 percent of the children of divorce are never visited by their fathers. Research has also shown that the pattern of visitation shaped during the first eighteen months after divorce is likely to continue through the years.

If the father is uninvolved and does not visit, both mother and child may feel heartbroken. Kathy related, "I still get upset realizing that my daughter doesn't know her dad or even what a daddy is. I wish my child could simply know the love and discipline and protection of a *father*." Anna, seventeen, said, "I feel so unhappy when Dad forgets to call, birthdays, holidays."

Ironically, it may be the father who cares the most who visits the least. Fathers who were very involved in the lives of their children before the divorce may cope with their pain by staying away. But the children, of course, conclude, as Brett did, that "he doesn't care enough to come to see us." And Dad's explanation makes no sense. Said Brett, "I don't understand. He says he does it because he loves us, but, to me, I think he should—it would help if he did—come around instead of staying away. Staying away makes it worse!"

For kids like Brett, the father-child relationship is understandably laden with painful feelings of rejection. What is surprising is the recent discovery that many kids whose fathers visit consistently and regularly also feel the same way.

In her interviews with children ten years after divorce, Judith Wallerstein discovered that the feeling of having "lost" one's father was unrelated to how often the father visited the child. While most of the fathers felt they had "done reasonably well in fulfilling their obligations," three-quarters of the children felt rejected by them. Wallerstein's conclusion was, *"What counts is not the quantity of time but the extent to which the father and child have been able to maintain a relationship in which the child feels valued."*[5] When father and child spend time together, but neither touches the other emotionally in more than a superficial way, the child experiences loss and hurt.

Helping her child cope with those kinds of feelings is one of the hardest tasks any single mother faces. Trying to convince the child that Daddy really does care is futile. Secondhand assurances from Mom can never take the place of a meaningful relationship with Dad. Author and pastor Gary Chapman has suggested that a mother might gently probe children for clues about what specifically makes them feel that Dad is distant or no longer cares. The mother can then relate these things to the father and suggest a way the father might communicate his love to the children.[6] Since the father may feel guilty or defensive about his postdivorce parenting, it is very important for the mother to plan a way to do this gently, being sure to make only *suggestions,* not demands.

Research shows that whether a father does or does not play an active role in his child's life, the role of a custodial mother is vital. Since she is the only full-time parent the child has, her mental health and the quality of her parenting combine to be "the single most important protective factor in a child's psychological development and well-being over the years."[7]

WHEN MOM BAILS OUT

There seems to be plenty of evidence that men do just as well as women when it comes to solo parenting, and that the children fare just as well with Dad as they do with Mom. (One exception, according to some experts, might be children under six who are well-bonded with their mothers.) One study found that, for six- to eleven-year-olds, it may actually be preferable for boys to be in the father's custody. Researchers James C. Young and Muriel E. Hamilton wrote, "Parenting skills, like most other skills, are basically learned behaviors, not biological endowments,"[8] their point being that men and women are equally capable and competent to parent.

Yet when it comes to assuming the roles of both Mom and Dad, single dads face different problems than their female counterparts.

Presenting . . . Mr. Mom

One of a man's biggest challenges in single parenting comes with the realization that he was not socialized to fill a mothering role. At best, most married men function as "mothers' helpers" when it comes to childcare and homemaking. Consequently, after divorce, few men are adequately prepared for the responsibilities of running a household and meeting all of their children's physical and emotional needs. When they receive custody of their children, they enter uncharted waters: Should my son be talking by now? How do I potty train? When will my daughter start her period, and what do I tell her? How do you bring down a fever? How do you sew on buttons? Roast a chicken? Buy children's clothing? Many men have never encountered these issues before.

When mothers meet a parenting or homemaking problem they have never encountered before, they rely on one another for help. Most mothers have a social network of women friends and relatives with whom they talk over questions and problems. They compare notes and learn from one another, comfortable in this mutually supportive role.

While the number of single fathers is growing, they are still relatively few and far between. Many do not know even one other man in their situation. Since there may be no other man to compare notes with, most single dads survive on advice from female friends and relatives. But, according to Steve, who has a son and a daughter, that's the easy part. He said, "The hardest part is when they have a mother-daughter banquet at church and Carla doesn't have a mother. And when they ask for the mothers to come in and help out at school, the kids don't have a mother. I would say that's the hardest part: not having the other half of your family there to be what they're supposed to be."

On the positive side, single parenting is likely to bring about a new depth to the relationship between a man and his children. One father said, "If anything positive has come out of this, it is day-to-day intimacy. I was too busy to spend this kind of time with my children before. There's no other way in the world that I would have sat down with my kids to fold the laundry."[9] Said Brandon, "I feel inside as if it's pretty neat to be a father and to be able to do all this—to kind of be a mother. I feel as if I'm closer to them now than I would be if I were still married."

Work

Full-time child rearing can put a strain on one of a man's primary sources of personal identity and fulfillment, his job. Like single mothers, custodial fathers may have to take time off when their children are sick or out of school, but they are less likely to meet with understanding from superiors and co-workers. If a promotion means having to travel, he may have to turn it down. If it means transferring to a new community, it may be out of the question if it means leaving relatives who are an important source of support and child care.

Even though single dads may find that family responsibilities limit their career advancement, most are considerably better off financially than single mothers. Unlike most mothers, a single dad can probably afford to hire baby-sitters or household help. This gives men an advantage in pursuing a social life and recreational activities.

JOINT CUSTODY?

Recognizing the fact that a child still needs interaction with both parents and that both parents are still fully parents, many have touted joint custody as the next best thing to an intact home.

In a joint custody arrangement children spend part of their time in the mother's home and part in the father's. With preschoolers, this can be an every-other-day arrangement, while older children might stay three days with one and four days with the other. Arrangements can also be divided weekly or even yearly. The idea of sharing the physical and legal custody of children seems fair and beneficial to everyone. The benefits to the adults are numerous. With a divided load, each parent can count on free time to pursue schooling or hobbies and enjoy recreation and socializing.

During the 1980s joint custody became so popular that courts at times impose it upon couples who actually prefer and agree upon a sole custody arrangement. Sometimes joint custody works well. Research also shows that joint custody fathers are more likely than noncustodial fathers to provide for their children material support and resources, including medical and dental care, gifts, clothes, and help with homework.

But sometimes joint custody doesn't work. When it does not, the results for children can be disastrous. In a 1991 interview with the *Wall Street Journal,* the chairman of the American Bar Association's family law section, Gary Skoloff, called joint custody "an experiment that failed."[10]

Professionals have always been divided as to the merits of joint custody. Of late, however, joint custody has fallen into much disfavor not only with attorneys, but with psychologists and parents themselves.

Joint custody often fails for the same reasons the marriage failed; the former spouses remain locked in conflict. Coparenting from separate camps calls for more cooperation and compromise than many couples could muster when they were under one roof. When the parental war is not resolved by divorce, the divorce has served no practical purpose, and the ongoing conflict, not the living arrangement, is harmful to the children. Those who are continually caught in the crossfire are psychologically wounded by the skirmishes that continue through the years.

One study noted that when parents cooperate with each other, adolescent children "seem to benefit." But "dual residence arrangements, however, do appear harmful when parents remain in high conflict."[11]

Still, the concept of joint custody—the freedom and flexibility it affords single parents—is worthy of consideration. For a few extraordinary families, it can and does work. But it requires sincere effort, flexibility, and a spirit of cooperation, commodities often in short supply after a decree of divorce. When these are lacking, joint custody can do more harm than good to the children involved.

SUGGESTIONS FOR PARENTS: GOING IT SOLO

1. Your friendships with men and women can have a positive influence on your children—by exposing them to adult conversation and male-female differences. Frequently inviting couples or single friends of both sexes for dinner and family fellowship can be one way to expose children to the complementary yet contrasting differences in men and women.

2. Children need to collaborate on tasks with adults of their same sex and receive praise and encouragement from adults of the opposite sex. See that your children have positive input and happy times with adults of their sex. Single mothers whose sons have all female school teachers and Sunday school teachers, for example, may want to consider enrolling sons in programs such as Boy Scouts.

13
Prescription for Parents

It is my goal that when my children are grown adults, their childhood will not have messed up their lives. They're going to be the fullest and the richest that they can possibly be because of their childhood.

—Sandy, thirty-seven, single mother of three

Because it changes family relationships in a permanent way, divorce forever changes the lives of those whom it touches. Children, because they are more dependent on family relationships than adults, are more vulnerable when those relationships change. If, as has been suggested, "life is relationships," then from the point of divorce onward, life itself takes on a different hue.

Researchers have pointed out that divorce creates relationships across the generations that have no counterpart in the intact family. Relationships with "no counterpart" can include any or all of these: one parent living apart from the child, maintaining a visiting relationship or dropping entirely out of the picture; a child spending three days in one parent's home and four days in the other parent's home; one or both parents bringing a boyfriend or girlfriend into the family circle; a third or fourth authoritative adult—stepparents; three or four sets of grandparents. If life is relationships, it can be said with certainty that life changes after divorce.

How a child handles both life and relationships after divorce may hinge on how sensitively the parents handle the divorce and its aftermath. Psychologist Steven E. Goldston told *Business Week,* "The parents—their attitudes and how they treat the kids from the first word spoken about separation to the awkward 'visitation' stage—can mean the difference between night and day to a toddler or a teenager."[1]

TELLING CHILDREN

The recollection of being told that one's parents plan to divorce is likely to be a moment in time forever frozen in a child's memory. Ten-year-old Ben recounted,

> I remember the day I found out my parents were getting a divorce. I had spent the night at a friend's house because my sister was having a slumber party. I came home to see if I could go to my friend's grandpa's house. My mom told me about the divorce and I cried for about fifteen minutes and went with my friend to his grandpa's to see if it would take away some of my feelings. That night I had completely forgotten it. The next night I remembered. I stayed up all night crying that night and two nights after.

Kimberlee, twelve, was seven when her parents separated. She recalled,

> My father told me, "Now don't you cry when I tell you this," and we had no idea what was coming. He had me and my sister on each side of him. He had already told my brother about it. I thought my sister was going to run out of the room, she was crying so hard. I thought, *How could he tell us this right now?* I mean, the way things were going right then. He said, "I don't love your mother anymore, and we're going to be separated for a while, so you won't be able to see me." I couldn't believe what he was saying. I was almost furious after a while.

Sarah, fifteen, said,

> I was sitting in the car with my mom. I remember . . . first it was shock, and then I started crying. That's just something I'll never forget and it still hits me sometimes and it upsets me.

The news that parents plan to divorce is never good news. Predictably, most children will respond with shock, anger, denial, tears, and protest. By planning exactly how and when to tell their children, parents can help soften the impact their disclosure is sure to have. Judith Wallerstein said, "Parents should take very seriously what they say to their children and how they say it, for what they say or fail to say will long be remembered."[2]

Here is a compilation of suggestions, recommended by Wallerstein[3] and other experts.

1. *Tell children about the divorce a week or two before the actual separation occurs.* This may cause an uncomfortable interim period, but it will make the break easier for children to accept. When possible, a couple should try to time their separation so as not to coincide with other major events. For example, parents could put off their separation until children have made a transition to a new school, recuperated from an operation, or passed a big exam.

2. *Choose a good time to tell them.* Don't spring the news when children's friends are present or when they are tired or cranky or when tension between parents is running high. Select a time for this critical disclosure when family members are feeling calm and will be able to talk without interruption.

3. *Tell all the children at the same time.* This way children will be able to support one another.

4. *Both parents should tell the children together, if possible.* This way neither Mom nor Dad is left looking like "the bad guy."

5. *Be honest.* This does not mean that children should be told all the sordid details, but they do deserve to know why their parents are breaking up.

6. *Be specific about the changes that will occur.* Children need to be told where each parent will be living, whether they will have to change schools, who will care for them, how often they will see the parent who is leaving, and any other important information that can be given. On the positive side, also tell them the things that will stay the *same*.

7. *Incorporate these ideas into what you say:*
   — Use the word *courage*. Tell them every family member will need to be brave as they face what lies ahead.
   — Express sadness. This gives children freedom to grieve and express their feelings.
   — Emphasize that the children are not responsible for your decision. (The read-aloud story at the end of this book may give you some ideas about how to do this.)
   — Present divorce as a solution. Tell them you have come to this decision reluctantly, as a last resort after trying many other things.
   — Assure them that both parents will continue to love the children and will take care of them.
   — Tell them you are sorry for the hurt the divorce will cause them.
   — Let children make suggestions; take their comments seriously, since their lives will be affected by the decisions made. This will also help alleviate some of their sense of powerlessness.

When a spouse leaves suddenly or when the divorce is bitter or impulsive, the task of telling the children may fall on one parent. He or she must not only break the news, but also explain the absence of the other parent. Under these circumstances the parent may be tempted to be less than honest. Brandon recalled,

> The first thing I told them was that their mother had to be away for a little bit—that she was sick and had to be away. I felt that was something they could understand at their age. They knew what it was to be sick. This is what I said until I realized that the situation didn't seem to be turning around.
>
> When we first separated, I thought there was a chance it wouldn't be permanent. That's what really made it hard. I didn't know what to tell them. I had talked with counselors and the doctor. They said that . . . [kids] can see right through you if you're not leveling with them. They told me it was better to tell them the truth, that they could handle that better than if I tried to make up all kinds of stories.
>
> After I realized that we were going to move toward divorce, I started telling them that Mommy was never going to live here

again, and that sort of thing. I used the word *divorce* and said we wouldn't be married anymore. Even now I still have to keep reinforcing that this is the way it's going to be because they still fantasize once in a while: "Mommy's coming home again," and that sort of thing. I continue to tell them we're not married anymore, and I talk about the future.

Sandy remembered,

The kids saw that something was going on, but I really didn't say anything to them. When it came time that they had to know, I knew the best thing to do was to be honest. The thing that parents do not realize is that if you aren't honest with kids, if you don't tell them the truth, then the only thing they can do is imagine. And usually, if they imagine, it's the worst or the wrong thing. I knew that the key thing was that the kids needed to know that it had nothing to do with them. It had absolutely nothing to do with them.

SOFTENING THE IMPACT OF DIVORCE

For Parents

Few people *like* divorce or being divorced. One does not walk to the marriage altar intending to end up in a divorce court. But it happens. For many, divorce is an act of desperation, the only apparent solution to an intolerable situation. For others it is a horrid, unwelcome surprise. Either way, regret and sorrow take up residence in the divorced person's heart.

Many parents feel that divorce places them at a proverbial location "between a rock and a hard place." On one hand, the divorce is now a fact, a done deal. On the other hand, because they are parents, they turn back the clock and worry, *Should we have stayed together for the sake of the children?*

Experts are divided on the issue of staying together for the sake of the children. John Guidubaldi, the director of the National Impact of Divorce Research study, says it's best for couples to stay together for the children. Guidubaldi's hope is that for the sake of the children "people will work harder to salvage their marriages."[4] Judith Wallerstein, however, says that children in highly conflicted marriages adjust less well than those whose parents divorce. She wrote, ". . . it is not useful to provide children with a model of adult behavior that avoids problem solving and that stresses martyrdom, violence or apathy. A divorce undertaken thoughtfully and realistically can teach children how to confront serious life problems with compassion, wisdom, and appropriate action."[5]

Current research is uncovering (1) that older children who have lived for years in an unhealthy, unnurturing family environment are more harmed than children whose parents divorce when they are very young and (2) that what went on in the family before the divorce can have a more lasting influence on a child than the divorce itself.

Neither parental divorce nor parental conflict has a positive effect on children. Either path brings hardship and pain. The ideal approach, and the biblical one, would be for the adults to seek a resolution to their difficulties and healing for their relationship. This may mean seeking professional or pastoral help and any other help mandated by a given situation. It may mean investing time and money. It may mean struggle and tears.

There is no question but that a reconciliation is superior to divorce, nor is there question about God's ability to provide help and healing. It is possible to salvage a dying marriage; many couples have returned from the brink of divorce, with God's help, and are glad today that they didn't give up on each other too soon.

Many couples divorce in haste, only to regret the decision later. Some few decide to try again and renew their commitment, having realized what is at stake for both them and their children. Reconciling a marriage after divorce is rare. Yet, when possible, it is clearly preferable and certainly biblical.

But when reconciliation is no longer possible, perhaps the best advice for parents is this: Don't look back. Don't spend time worrying about what you could have or should have done differently. Instead, make the most of the opportunities you have in the present. Move forward in a positive way, focusing on ways to build up your children and help them adjust well.

For Children

Researchers can now point to several factors common among children who have adjusted well after divorce. An understanding of these can be useful as parents seek ways to help their children after divorce. The news is positive—and exciting—because it means that the kind of parenting kids receive after divorce can really make a difference!
Kids who cope best:

1. Have parents who succeed in defusing the conflict between them. These divorcing parents keep their anger in check for the sake of their kids. They refuse to attack each other verbally or physically, and they cooperate with each other. A study by John Guidubaldi shows that when parental conflict is laid to rest, kids learn more in school and have fewer behavioral problems.

2. Have fathers who stay involved in their lives. Dads who participate in the upbringing of their sons and daughters, are available to them, and support them financially have children who do better academically and emotionally. These kids are more independent both at school and at play than other children of divorce.

3. Have close, healthy relationships with each parent. For boys, good overall adjustment is linked to the father-son relationship. For all children, a quality relationship with a psychologically stable custodial parent is vital.

4. Have strong, supportive relationships with adults who can serve as *mentors* to the child. These can be grandparents, coaches, teachers, stepparents, or anyone who cares about the child and shares a common interest. The interest, whether it is cooking, sports, building models, or playing the piano, is the keystone in a relationship where the child feels he or she is special and a person of worth.

It appears that relationships—between the parents, between parent and child, and between the child and others—hold the key to good adjustment.

Most parents would welcome mentors in the lives of their children. Similarly, once parents recognize that both mother and father are extremely important to a child's adjustment, they would likely encourage the child's relationship with a former spouse. But when it comes to establishing a good relationship with one's ex-husband or wife, many people run into trouble. Yet making peace with the child's other parent is vital to the child's well-being. But how?

SUCCESSFUL DIVORCE

Someone has said, "If you were not able to make the marriage work, then at least make the divorce work." Presumably the purpose of divorce is to alleviate the stress and unhappiness in the family and allow everyone to get on with life. But when arguing and conflict continue on after divorce, no one benefits, least of all the children. One psychologist has gone so far as to label the strain that warring parents put on a child as a "form of child abuse."[6]

For the sake of the children, both parents must lay down their weapons; no one stands to gain anything from prolonging the conflict. It goes without saying that this is no small task; if it were easy, many couples would still be married. I offer two suggestions to single parents in this regard. These are not simple suggestions. Each requires maturity and courage.

Establish a code of conduct. Resolve to abide by certain standards of behavior in your relationship with your ex-partner, not because it is easy to do so, but because doing so is in the best interests of your child. Put your resolution in writing. Discuss the contents with the other parent and see if you can agree on the basics. Here are some essential ingredients:

I/we resolve:
- to make no negative statements about the other parent when children are present
- to shield children from anger and conflict
- to refrain from verbal and physical attacks on the other parent

- never to employ children as weapons—asking them to "spy," relay messages, ask for child support checks, or do anything that places them in an unfair position between parents.

Grieve and forgive. When we cling to bitterness or resentment, the wrong done to us plays through our minds over and over, like a continuous-loop tape. Each time the offense crosses our consciousness, it hurts us afresh and etches deeper into our memories. We are miserable until we snip the tape with forgiveness. Failure to forgive results in wounds that never heal. After divorce, a lack of forgiveness can inject poison into a child's relationship with his or her other parent. Forgiveness is God's will, surely in part because he does not want us to inflict ourselves and others with emotional pain again and again.

Until we forgive, we are unable to help our children to forgive. We must set the example. Until we forgive, the emotional and psychological freedom that our children might otherwise gain may never come.

But how do you forgive?

I am convinced that many of us make a big mistake when a hurting person comes to us for comfort and support. We say the answer is forgiveness, but we ignore the person's pain and wounds. It is a little like driving down the highway and happening onto the scene of an accident. We pull over and run to the aid of the victims. A woman crawls from the wreckage, bleeding badly and crying. It looks as though her arm may be broken. We rush to her side and say, "You know, what you need to do is forgive the other driver." Then we get back in our car and drive away.

Ridiculous? Of course. Yet when the injuries are on the inside instead of the outside of a person, this is exactly the way many of us, even some in the helping professions, treat those wounded by divorce or other traumatic experiences.

What was said at the scene of the accident was true: The woman does need to forgive the other driver. But she also needs help from someone who will care for her and not deny that she has been injured. Before she can get to the point of forgiveness, she may need a blood transfusion, a cast on her arm, and a shoulder to cry on.

The wounds of divorce are real, even though they may be invisible to everyone but the person who suffered the injury. Divorce is a loss of the greatest magnitude, and the stages of grief are a form of emotional first aid; we must give ourselves— and others—permission to grieve. Part of grief is allowing oneself to feel anger. Part of grief is tears. Part of grief is being honest with ourselves and God about what we feel. And part of grief may be talking those feelings out with a safe person—a good friend or a professional therapist. But at the end of grief, there comes a time to forgive.

Romans 12:18 says, "If it is possible, as far as it depends on you, live at peace with everyone." If we believe in the Lord Jesus Christ, we are under a mandate to forgive (Romans 12:19– 21; Matthew 6:14–15; Ephesians 4:32; Colossians 3:13). Your former spouse may or may not do the same. God will not hold you responsible for what your ex-spouse does or does not do. But when you forgive, you are kept from destroying yourself. And you fortify your children's opportunity for a good adjustment.

Forgiveness means making a conscious, willful decision no longer to harbor resentment against an ex-spouse. It means affirming before God that you no longer wish to hold anything against him or her. Negative feelings and bad memories will rise up to challenge your decision to forgive, but with God's help, each day can be more victorious than the last. If forgiveness is difficult, I encourage you to seek out pastoral counseling or professional therapy.

THROUGH THE EYES OF CHILDREN

Children are astute observers of parental behavior. They are uncannily perceptive and can be scathingly critical or quite complimentary and appreciative. Usually they strive to be fair, carefully weighing mitigating circumstances in their own minds. Above all, they are candid. They have strong feelings about divorce, about their families, and about what their parents have done right or wrong in handling the breakup. In the end, they are the final authorities on what it means to be a child of divorce; they are our best teachers.

The following is a potpourri of comments children have shared with me, both positive and negative, regarding Mom, Dad, and family life after divorce. Think about the circumstances and feelings that lie behind their words.

"I'm happy that both my parents still love me."

"My father is a nice guy, but he has built resentment against my mom."

"My family has always been there for me when I needed a helping hand or a shoulder to lean on."

"My father needs to understand that for a relationship of any kind to exist, you need to show genuine concern about the other person's needs, desires, and expectations. For me to take his suggestions seriously, he must show—not tell—a concern for my life."

"I'm happy that my parents get along fairly well. It makes it easier on us kids."

"What upsets me most about my parents' divorce is that my father, who originally wanted a divorce from my mother, now regrets it."

"My father is such a gentle, loving man. He was always a good provider and spent time with us. He had trouble expressing himself, which I am sure led to many of my parents' arguments. My mother left one day, taking nothing with her. It was sad. A lot of loneliness took her place. My dad didn't talk about it, which made it even worse because we never knew how he felt."

"Our family is close, considering the circumstances, but sometimes resentful. We argue too often."

"Mom never claimed to be perfect. She knew she had made mistakes in her marriage, but by the time she knew what they were it was too late."

"I wish my parents would get back together and stop fighting."

"I wish my father would come and visit me, but he can't."

"It upsets me that my parents are not friends and don't have any communication between them."

"The hardest part about having divorced parents is they always fight."

"Our family has to deal with a lot of problems that can be traced back to the separation of my parents."

"I got extremely mad when my dad was separated from Mom and he came and asked her for sexual favors. He'd come over for lunch and then they'd go back into the bedroom. That used to make me so mad, and it still does when I think about it."

"Mother understood that no good could come from downing my father in front of the kids. She always said she could see where she had failed as well as my father. Although she may have had very bitter feelings, she never passed them on to us."

14
Family Heirlooms

My grandfather had been married about six times; my parents have been divorced. I think about it all the time. It's scary. It could happen to me, too. Because after my dad and his dad, I think it runs in the family.

—Brett, age fifteen

Several years ago, The *Winston-Salem Journal* invited children of divorce to write in, answering two questions: "Has divorce affected you?" and "What would you tell a friend whose parents were getting a divorce?" A young woman named Debbi responded this way:

My parents were divorced when I was 3. I've had no family life to speak of. There were custody fights, suicide attempted, two stepfathers, not to mention being tossed from relative to relative. It was not unusual to change schools three times in one year.

To top it all off, my parents could not stand to be in the same room. You can see that my graduation and wedding were lacking in loved ones. It has been as if I had to choose between them all my life.

I am now almost 26, happily married and have two children. You would think I made it pretty well to have come from a broken home. However, I find that my problems are just starting. . . .

My responsibilities at home were many, including keeping my sister and later stepbrother and stepsister. That carried over into my motherhood, giving me problems with feeling trapped. Sometimes I feel I've kept kids all my life. I believe my husband is a good father—or at least my idea of one. I don't really know much about fathers; mine was never around.

The real pain came when I realized my children were going through the same thing. Three sets of grandparents is hard enough to explain, without the complication of two of them being so immature that they can't be in the same room. The children began to think the missing grandparent doesn't love them. Boy, does that ever sound familiar! I feel my children have become a little unsure of our own home life because of this.

There is no good way to handle it because divorce isn't good. It does help to have parents who don't shut you out and do communicate with each other. My faith has been a great comfort.

My message to all parents who are thinking of divorce, is not to. At least try everything before you do. (That should take you a couple of years!) . . . If you feel you can't make it, keep in mind you are divorcing each other, not your children.

You owe it to them to at least be civil to each other. Divorce affects not just the two of you, but your children and their children and their children.[1]

When a couple loses hope, believing they are at an unresolvable impasse, the divorce that results can have effects that follow their children into adulthood, as they grow up, marry, and begin families of their own.

This reality was evident in many conversations I had with young adults whose parents have divorced. Life is not compartmentalized into sterile segments labeled "childhood," "adolescence," and "adulthood." Rather, life is one continuous strand, with each stage blending seamlessly into the next. Childhood flows into the teen years; teenagers grow into adults. And the family experiences of childhood accompany us though all of life, silently coloring romance, marriage, and parenthood. Childhood is but a template from which adulthood is drawn.

This truth often comes as a shock to many children of divorce and dysfunctional families. They grow up, marry, and have children, hoping to establish a new life and leave the past far behind. But what they often find instead is that their problems, in Debbi's words, "are just beginning." To their chagrin, they find, as thirty-year-old Kristie found: ". . . it affects my relationship with my husband as well." And sooner or later they discover something that at first seems impossible. In Debbi's words again, "Divorce affects not just the two of you, but your children and their children and their children."

Debbi may not realize it, but her insights illustrate a profound biblical truth. And, with so many Christian marriages splintering in divorce, her words also raise some questions that trouble many sincere believers: Why do we have so much trouble loving each other? Why do we struggle so in our efforts to treat one another according to biblical principles—the principles that make marriage work?

I see a two-part answer to those questions. The first part goes all the way back to the Garden of Eden. The reason for our struggle in marriage is rooted in the reason Cain killed Abel: the sinful, inherently selfish nature of humanity.

This is no news to Christians; our sinfulness is the reason Christ came to earth to die. Our fallen nature put a barricade between us and God. The shed blood of Christ, applied to individual hearts, takes away the barricade. Apart from Christ, we have no access to God, no access to heaven. It was a problem we could never have solved on our own.

But Christ is more than just our ticket to heaven. Christianity is relevant to everyday life, every day. As our indwelling Savior, Christ becomes to us an endless source and resource. He gives us knowledge of the will of God as we read the Bible. He gives us both power and desire to do what is right. He loves us, guides us, teaches us, cares for us with a perfect knowledge of what we need.

Why, then, do we have so much trouble loving one another, making marriages work?

Some might say the issue is obedience: Christians choose whether or not they will obey God; we choose how we will treat members of our family. Others might cite our bent toward sin; even the most sincere and godly believer makes mistakes in dealing with others. Certainly we all fail and sin against people we love. But can these alone account for the failure of so many marriages? Or is something else at work in our lives? Something so insidious that we fail to recognize it?

There is more. A great many people are now in the process of discovering the personal implications of Numbers 14:18: "The

Lord is slow to anger and abundant in lovingkindness, forgiving iniquity and transgression; but He will by no means clear the guilty, visiting the iniquity of the fathers on the children to the third and fourth generations" (NASB).

If I understand this verse correctly, it does not mean that God punishes children and grandchildren for sins committed by their predecessors. Rather, it means that God does not step in and alter the natural consequences of sin as they filter down through the generations.

Divorce, unquestionably, is rooted in sin—but not always just our own sin. Each generation is linked to the one before and after it. Sin can be confessed and forgiven, but its effects can still travel through the generations. We are affected by the morality, choices, and lifestyles of our parents, grandparents, and great-grandparents.

The principle works positively as well as negatively. Consider Psalm 103:17–18:

> *But from everlasting to everlasting*
> *the LORD's love is with those who fear him,*
> *and his righteousness with their children's children—*
> *with those who keep his covenant*
> *and remember to obey his precepts.*

What gets passed from one generation to the next is not tangible. Attitudes, values, moral standards, ideas about friendship, how children should be disciplined, how husbands and wives are to treat each other—these are not passed on as we might pass on Grandma's silver tea service. Instead, they are absorbed in the normal course of family life, internalized effortlessly and without conscious thought, as the years go by. By the time we are adults, they reside so deeply within us that we usually have difficulty recognizing why we behave as we do, think as we do, and expect the things we do.

Every family bequeaths both positive and negative attitudes and behaviors to its members. Families splintered by divorce, or burdened with serious problems, however, often bequeath some of the least desirable "heirlooms" to their offspring. Children carry them down the aisle on their wedding day, unaware of their presence.

Traumatic childhood experiences, which might relate to

divorce, alcoholism, abuse, or emotional repression, leave an imprint on the minds and hearts of children. Children with traumatic backgrounds may experience low self-esteem, repressed anger, feelings of abandonment, fear of authority figures, feelings of isolation, sexual repression, and a tendency to control others, to seek approval, and to be fearful.

Of course, not every divorce leaves the same imprint. Every situation, every network of relationships, is unique. Yet some of the common "heirlooms" of parental divorce are as follows:

PERSONAL LEGACY

Richard Kulka and Helen Weingarten, social psychologists at the Survey Research Center at the University of Michigan, did two studies—one in 1957 and one in 1976—designed to determine whether children of different generations responded differently to parental divorce. They concluded that while society had changed and divorce had increased, the way that children responded to divorce remained the same. Some of their findings:

- Between the ages of twenty-one and thirty-four, adults from divorced homes were less likely to be "very happy" and more likely to report symptoms of poor physical health

- At all ages, people from divorced homes were likely to
  - recall their childhoods as the unhappiest time in their lives
  - say they've been on the verge of a nervous breakdown
  - feel that bad things often happen to them
  - have troubled marriages
  - have a different outlook on the marital role than other people

- Men, especially, were more apt to experience feelings of anxiety[2]

Phillip Shaver and Carin Rubenstein, who conducted a Loneliness Research Project at New York University, found that adults from divorced homes were:

- Lonelier than other adults

- Lower in self-esteem than other adults
- More likely to have crying spells, insomnia, constant worry, feelings of worthlessness, guilt, and despair
- More likely to feel afraid, anxious, and angry when they were alone[3]

Other studies show that people from divorced homes have shorter life expectancies, are more likely to have dropped out of school, and are more likely to have run away from home.

Fear of Marital Commitment

Eighteen-year-old Carol said of her parents, "It scares me when I think that two people who thought they were in love enough to marry now hate each other." Melodie expressed bewilderment "that after twenty-six years of marriage and bringing seven children into the world a marriage could go bad." Observing the dissolution of a marriage that once seemed so permanent and secure can at the very least cause a child to become more hesitant about making such a personal commitment.

A child may conclude that if commitment ultimately results in being hurt, it is best not to set oneself up for it. For reasons of his own, nine-year-old Tim has already decided, "I am not going to get married."

Those who marry may consciously or unconsciously refrain from making a full emotional investment in the marriage, to the obvious hurt of the spouse. In so doing they may sow the very seeds that will eventually result in their own divorce.

Choosing the Wrong Mate

The desire to marry a man "just like Daddy" or a woman "just like the girl who married dear old Dad" is not unusual. After all, parents are a child's primary source of information about what a husband is, what a wife is, and what marriage means. Children of divorce, however, may find themselves caught up in patterns that confuse their mate-selection process and virtually guarantee their unhappiness, since they may still be dealing with unresolved issues from childhood.

Dr. Robert S. Weiss, a professor of sociology at the

University of Massachusetts and a lecturer at Harvard Medical School, has said that children of divorce tend to commit themselves to unpromising relationships that mirror their parents' breakup; even in the most promising relationships, such children focus not on the present happy times or dream about a future together but on the breakup they feel sure is to come.[4]

When Dad leaves home, daughters of divorce sometimes grow up thinking of themselves as covictims along with their mothers. Some speculate that having "lost" in an emotional sense as children, these women continue to view themselves as losers, expecting to lose in other emotional relationships. As a result they are attracted to men who are unable to meet their emotional needs and who will abandon them or treat them as their fathers did.[5]

An unplanned pregnancy can affect a mate-choice. As we have already noted, teens and preteens from divorced homes are more likely to be sexually active and to have more partners than other teens. Whether they are simply seeking comfort following divorce or trying to substitute sex for a missing parent's love, pregnancy catches many by surprise. The result is often a marriage that may easily result in divorce within a few years. One-third of the divorcing couples studied by Dr. Wallerstein had rushed into marriage because of an unplanned pregnancy. On the average, these marriages lasted eight years.

Excess Baggage

Children of divorce and those from highly conflicted intact homes tend to develop a negative outlook on home and family. Endless parental combat can drain the endearment from words like *father, mother, family,* and *marriage.* Children define these words on the basis of their own experiences, which may be vastly incongruous with the experiences of other children.

Christian children of divorce know two definitions for each of these words: the way things are supposed to be, as defined by the Bible and the Christian subculture of which they are a part, and the way things have turned out to be in their particular corner of the real world. Trying to reconcile both definitions can be confusing and painful. A sermon on "the Christian home" can be hard to bear, because the child knows he or she supposedly *had* a Christian home—but something wasn't right. Sorting through what was and what ought to have been is necessary to establish what kind of a spouse and parent he or she will become.

A young person who marries before that sorting and healing process is completed will likely carry some excess baggage into the marital relationship. If the bride's parents dealt with the conflict that led to their divorce by slamming doors, she will no doubt have a good idea of how she will behave at the first sign of disagreement. If the groom's parents were in the habit of sweeping the problems that led to their divorce under the rug, somewhere in his baggage there is probably a broom of the same make and model.

All of us tend to reproduce the kind of family environment in which we grew up. Children of divorce are likely to have internalized patterns of communication and conflict resolution that will probably be as counterproductive for them as they were for their parents.

Young adults from divorced homes may also carry in their baggage an inordinate number of emotional needs that they unrealistically expect their spouses to be able to meet. They may view their spouses more as surrogate parents than as partners, expecting them to pick up where negligent parents left off. Their need for security, nurture, and attention may be far more than the spouses are able or willing to supply—burdening the marriages from the outset.

Parenting Patterns

"Most people do what they do out of habit, not because of rational considerations. Parents behave toward their children by and large in the same way their parents behaved toward them," write researchers Young and Hamilton.[6] Over the years studies have proven rather conclusively that this tends to be the case, and this is precisely why children of divorce sometimes grow up confused about how to parent their own children.

A person who suffered inattention from an overly busy or unconcerned parent naturally has trouble learning to express love and care for others, including his or her own children. Dr. James Mallory has written, "When we take genetics and environment into consideration, it is not surprising that there are atheists who are more loving than Christians. A person's theological position is not the only variable related to love."[7]

Divorce can affect not only one's concept of parenting, but also expectations about what a coparent is supposed to do. Twelve-year-old Kimberlee remarked, "Most of the time, with divorced parents, the mother gets the children because the father is the one fooling around and doing all that other stuff. So, if the father gets the children, most of the time it's an unhappy place." Her experience? "The way my dad acted, they almost put him in jail because he wouldn't pay the child support." Kimberlee has already formed some definite opinions about fathers, which she has generalized from her own father's behavior: Mothers are responsible and fathers aren't. Mothers care; fathers don't. People who have had little or no contact with their fathers may have fewer notions about what a partner's role should be: As Debbi commented, "I believe my husband is a good father—or at least my idea of one. I don't really know much about fathers; mine was never around."

The experience of parental divorce may be a determining factor in the decision not to become a parent at all. Those who approach adulthood still feeling great emotional neediness may choose to forgo child rearing completely. They may fear they will only visit the pain of their childhoods on another generation. Biller reported, "Women who rejected the feminine role of wife and mother were more likely to come from broken homes than were women who accepted these roles."[8]

Divorce as an Option

E. Mavis Hetherington has predicted that three out of four children of divorce will one day get divorced.[9] More recently, statistics show that divorce does, in fact, tend to run in families. As has been noted already, white American women whose parents were divorced have an incidence of divorce 60 percent higher than the general population. And all children of divorce are at increased risk of getting divorced themselves, according to accumulating statistics.[10]

Ironically, those who have experienced parental divorce as children are usually the most determined to keep their own marriages together. They vow never to put their children through the ordeal of divorce, yet they find themselves repeating family history.

Jonathan said,

> My divorce was unique for me because I had married "for life" and had not anticipated a marriage failure. It was especially hurtful for me because as a child I had been deprived of a normal family relationship and my goal in life was to be a good husband and father. Sometimes I wonder why I waited so long to get married—because I wanted a lasting relationship—only to have it dissolve with so much pain and bitterness.

The children who shared with me their thoughts about marrying one day were resolute in their determination never to divorce. Benjamin, ten, vowed, "I will try and work everything out with my wife and try to stay together 'till death do we part.'" Twelve-year-old Paul was typical of many when he said, "I would not want my family to go through what I went through." Eight-year-old Mary Beth stated, "When I get married someday I will stay married." Brett, fifteen, said, "I'd try everything not to let it happen."

Teenagers like Brett often feel just as strongly as younger children about not divorcing, but they have an inkling, perhaps, that having experienced parental divorce places them at a disadvantage. Jennifer's statement, quoted in an earlier chapter, bears repeating:

> For me, as a Christian, divorce is not an option. However, it will be difficult for me, because of my parents' divorce, to try and remember that divorce is not an option. I am afraid that when my husband and I have a fight I will think that the only solution is divorce. This feeling comes from seeing my father get married and divorced three times.

REAL TRUTH BRINGS REAL HEALING

Something very positive is beginning to happen. In our generation, perhaps more than ever before, people are beginning to recognize a connection between what is happening in their lives today and the way their parents and grandparents lived.

They realize that their families were unable to equip them for success in marriage and other relationships. Many, in fact, were instead "programmed" for failure. Many Christians are now comfortable with the understanding that eternal salvation and emotional health are two different things. The marvelous link between the two lies in the fact that it is Jehovah Rapha ("the Lord That Healeth") who personally guides us into emotional wholeness. It is El-Shaddai ("Giver of Strength") who enables us to lay aside denial, face the truth about how deeply wounded we are, and humbly seek honesty with ourselves and with God— "truth in the inner parts," as described in Psalm 51:6.

Divorce ends a marriage, but it does not solve the problems we carry inside. They will accompany us into our next relationship; they will follow our children into their marriages. But the damage of divorce can be minimized if we seek help; the kind of help we need depends on the severity of the injury.

If you cut yourself with a paring knife while peeling potatoes, the wound hurts. It bleeds. You might even shed a few tears. But you probably don't need a doctor. You know how to take care of yourself, and the wound gets better.

But if you cut your fingers on a power saw, you head straight for the hospital. Your hand hurts terribly. You lose considerable blood. And you certainly cry. You know that Band-Aids and Bactine are not enough for an injury like this. Your focus is not on whether you can "afford" to seek help, but on what might happen if you don't.

Emotional injuries, like physical ones, vary in severity. All divorces are not equal in impact. While it is the adult relationship, the marriage, that sets the tone in the home, not every divorce represents a history of poor *parenting*. Even in a bad marriage the overall parenting received by the children may be good. This is to say that not every child of divorce needs therapy or counseling. Sometimes as we comfort ourselves and seek the comfort of God and friends, our wounds will heal over time. But when the trauma is very great, and when time and tenderness prove insufficient, we need to step outside the realm of our present resources and look for something more.

When our pain is emotional instead of physical, we often choose to endure our suffering. If we have subscribed to the false and dangerous notion that Christians have no problems, a feeling of shame may prevent us from seeking help. Or we may feel we "can't afford" to seek help for ourselves or our children. Sometimes, all things considered, we can't afford not to.

Because divorce causes both an emotional and a spiritual injury, it is best to seek help from someone who is both a skilled therapist and a committed Christian. Not many pastors, and not even all professional counselors, have the skill and training to work with the children or the adults of divorce. Choose carefully. If the best therapists in your area are non-Christians and you choose to go to one of them, it might be helpful to find a second individual such as a pastor to add a spiritual focus.

If you are able to identify family dysfunctions that led up to the divorce, seek a professional with special training in that area. For example, if a parent or grandparent had a drinking problem that damaged family relationships, a therapist specializing in adult children of alcoholics might be best able to help. Seek recommendations from others.

Ask questions about experience and training; ask about personal religious beliefs. Look for someone with whom you and/or your child can build trust and rapport. And look to God for guidance; he knows exactly what you need, and he is still in the business of working all things together for the good of those who love him (Romans 8:28).

Greek scholar Kenneth Wuest has written:

> Christian suffering, whether it be in the form of persecution because of a Christlike life, or whether it comes to us in the form of trials and testing which are the natural accompaniment of a Christlike life, such as illness, sorrow, or financial losses, is always used by a God of love to refine our lives. It burns out the dross, makes for humility, purifies and increases our faith, and enriches our lives. And like the goldsmith of old, God keeps us in the smelting furnace until He can see the reflection of the face of the Lord Jesus in our lives.[11]

Divorce is not good in and of itself. It was never part of God's perfect plan. Yet in his hand even the pain and hardships of divorce do not remain meaningless or purposeless. They are incorporated into God's plans, and those plans are always good.

" 'For I know the plans I have for you,' declares the LORD, 'plans to prosper you and not to harm you, plans to give you hope and a future' " (Jeremiah 29:11). By the grace of God, even divorce can help build Christlike character, an eternal heirloom that will never fade with age or time.

PART FIVE

HEALING PROPOSITIONS

15

A Pound of Cure: How Teachers, Friends, and Churches Can Help

If it hadn't been for my Christian friends, I probably would have done something stupid like try to commit suicide.

—Sarah, age fifteen

The words of Lamentations 5:1–3 could well be the cry of many modern children of divorce:

> *Remember, O LORD, what has happened to us;*
>   *look, and see our disgrace.*
> *Our inheritance has been turned over to aliens,*
>   *our homes to foreigners.*
> *We have become orphans and fatherless,*
>   *our mothers like widows.*

In many ways single parents and their children are modern-day equivalents to the widows and orphans to whom the Bible has much to say. The word for *orphan* in the verse above is *yathom*. In Hebrew it means "lonely" or "one deprived of one or both parents." This word seems appropriate to children of divorce; many are lonely; since most are rarely in the company of both parents at once, they are "deprived of one parent" much of the time.

Meeting the needs of widows and orphans has always been characteristic of God's people (2 Kings 4:1–7; Acts 6:1–3; 1 Timothy 5). Perhaps the time has come for us to expand our definitions to include those "widowed" and "orphaned" by divorce.

Following divorce, children confront frustration on all sides: Parents who are changing, fellow believers who do not comfort them, a legal system that is insensitive to their desires and needs, and teachers and friends who do not understand. Studies have shown that subtle stereotypes about children of divorce are common and that this bias can actually cause people to treat children differently after divorce. One study cautioned:

> If teachers, school principals, counselors, psychologists, social workers, and parents expect children from divorced families to have more than their share of problems, they may treat these children in ways that exacerbate, or even generate, these very problems. . . . The possibility of a self-fulfilling prophecy should be of concern to all people who deal with children from divorced families.[1]

The concern, of course, is that if others do not seem to value them or support them, children may begin to devalue themselves.

My fifteen-year-old friend Sarah told me, "I think I'm more open than some people are, but I know some kids who won't admit they need anything. But deep down inside they do need support from other people. And whether they admit it or not I think nine out of ten times they really welcome it." Opportunities for helping kids like Sarah and her friends vary depending on a number of factors. The kind of relationship one has with the child and the parents, the age of the child, one's level of concern and empathy, the amount of time one has in contact with the child, and the nature of that contact, all modify the kind of influence adults can have. For example, a teacher who sees the child five days a week has opportunities that an aunt or uncle in another city does not have, and vice versa.

Here are a few general guidelines for anyone who loves a child of divorce and wants to help meet any of his or her emotional, physical, or spiritual needs.

FIRST AID KIT

Keep in mind this "first aid kit" when you spend time with children of divorce.

1. *Listen.* Divorce is a crisis—probably the most traumatic event they have ever experienced. One of the most significant ways to help in a crisis is simply to give the gifts of a listening ear and a caring heart. If children are willing to talk, it is because they *need* to talk. They are probably not looking for pearls of wisdom as much as for a sympathetic listener. Even when we give children all the "right answers," they may still feel unsatisfied because explanations touch only the intellect. Deep emotional needs may call more for tenderness and concern than facts and logic.

2. *Make eye contact*—while you listen and when you talk. This leaves no doubt in the child's mind about whether he or she has your full attention. A child will feel assured that you care. It also helps a child like and trust you more.

3. *Sit on the child's level.* Counselors suggest that adults position themselves so that they are on the same eye-level as the child. The idea is to avoid talking down to someone, in a literal sense.

4. *Touch.* A hug, a brief touch on the arm, or an arm around the shoulders communicates sincere concern. Some studies have shown that when therapists touch their adult clients in such nonthreatening ways, they are more responsive to therapy. Kids know how to read a loving touch!

5. *Ask "what?" rather than "why?"* Children typically respond to a *why* question with "I don't know." But if you ask *what*—What is happening at home? What do you like to do after school?—you've asked a question a child can answer. And you've opened the way for conversation.

PITFALLS

Well-meaning adults sometimes make mistakes in reaching out to children. Here are some pitfalls to avoid. These are guaranteed *not* to help.

- Saying that big boys don't cry, or that he or she should grow up and stop being such a baby
- Suggesting that if the child's behavior has always been as bad as it is today, it's no wonder Dad left
- Speaking unkindly about either parent
- Pretending nothing has happened and offering no words of support
- Feeding a reconciliation fantasy with false hopes
- Encouraging the child to reject one parent or take sides
- Telling the child he or she is better off now that the parents are separated

HOW TEACHERS CAN HELP

Teachers are often the most constant adults in a child's life. And because children may already admire them, many teachers are in an ideal position to help during parental divorce.

Some schools maintain that a teacher's role is purely educational and that what happens in the child's personal life should be of no concern. Many teachers feel this way too, since they already have more than enough paperwork and student problems. Other schools and teachers take the approach that unless a child can somehow be helped to cope with personal problems, education will not occur; a child too exhausted, depressed, or distracted to concentrate or care won't learn.

Support Groups

Hundreds of schools now offer support groups for children whose parents are divorced. These are usually small groups of six to eight children close in age. They meet once or twice a week during lunch, recess, or after school to talk about concerns at home. In this safe environment they express feelings and draw strength from one another. The leader is usually the school psychologist or a specially trained teacher. Some groups are designed to be temporary, twelve to sixteen weeks. In other schools children can choose to participate for as long as they like; some stay involved for years; many see it as a club.

Teachers are enthusiastic about these groups. They say that

participants have fewer behavioral problems and do better academically. Teachers often notice that positive changes take place quickly as children begin to understand what happened to their families and realize that this has happened to others also.

For information about starting a school support group, write to:

Drew Lamden
Center for the Family in Transition
5725 Paradise Drive, Building B
Suite 300
Corte Madera, CA 94925
Phone: (415) 924-5750

or

Dr. Joanne Pedro-Carroll, Director
Children of Divorce Intervention Program
Center for Community Study
University of Rochester
575 Mount Hope Avenue
Rochester, NY 14620
Phone: (716) 275-2547

In-Class Help

Teachers who have freedom to work creatively with students concerning the topic of divorce may wish to incorporate the following ideas:

Plan a classroom discussion, or a series of discussions, on divorce. This can serve the same purpose as a support group for students whose parents are divorced. They will see that some classmates have the same problems they do. They can share ideas and ask questions of each other. Students from intact homes will gain understanding about their friends. It might be a good idea to send an informational note home to parents ahead of time, and to let the principal know your plans.

Teach "feeling" words. A child cannot verbalize emotions if he or she does not know the words that describe them. The right words can unlock feelings that need to come out.

Have age-appropriate reading materials in the classroom

that deal with the topic of divorce. Encourage students to ask questions about what they read.

One-on-One Help

Teachers may be unable to involve the whole class in a discussion about divorce, but one-on-one discussions can always be arranged. As a first step toward helping, define your own attitudes about divorce and be in touch with any negative feelings that might cloud your interaction with the child.

Apart from any divorce-related conversation, make an effort daily to speak to a child whose parents are divorcing. Even passing comments like "How's it going?" are enough to let the child know you have an interest. It may not seem significant, but many children are starved for adult attention at this time; it may mean a great deal to the child.

With regard to divorce, teacher-student conversation is best directed toward things within the context of a teacher-student relationship. The teacher will want to express a personal concern for the student and talk about how things at home might affect the child's schoolwork. A teacher might give suggestions about study habits or keeping grades up. If the student opens up, by all means be a good listener. He or she may be trusting you with thoughts and feelings never before brought out in the open.

Those who teach very young children might hold them on their laps during conversations. A teacher of older students might invite a child to talk privately during a study hall or after school. If you think the child would benefit, you can suggest he or she talk further with a school counselor.

What Kids Say

I asked my panel of experts how teachers could help kids through the difficult period surrounding parental divorce. Here are their thoughts.

MARY BETH: Understanding why I'm upset.
age eight

ANGELA: Not hollering at them for daydreaming, but giv-
age sixteen ing them that little extra bit of help and care.

BENJAMIN: Teaching them to handle their problems and
age ten: giving them a little extra attention.

KIMBERLEE: Treating them like other kids.
age twelve

ANNA: Listening. Kids need an objective, outside
age seventeen shoulder to lean on, other than family.

PAUL: Giving them advice on how to keep their
age twelve   grades up.

TIM: Telling them about divorced parents.
age nine

JENNIFER: Letting students know that they are available to
age seventeen talk about any problem.

CAROL: Not always assuming that kids live with both
age eighteen their mother and father.

Refer to chapter 8, "Report Card Blues," for additional insights concerning the way divorce affects a child at school.

HOW FRIENDS CAN HELP

Adult friends of the family can leave a lasting and valuable imprint on a child's life by providing emotional support and affirmation, financial or practical help, spiritual guidance, and just-for-fun times of recreation.

Judith Wallerstein's research showed that some of the children who adjusted best after divorce were those who had a *mentor*—an adult friend with whom they shared a common interest. This was a person who was able to influence the child intellectually, morally, and emotionally by virtue of the special relationship they enjoyed. Any common interest could be a springboard to this kind of special friendship.

If you enjoy some of the same activities as a child you are seeking to help, perhaps these can be the seeds that will grow into an extraordinary friendship.

I asked several single parents how they felt friends could help their children adjust to life after divorce.

SANDY:	Just love them. That's the most you can do for kids. And do things with them. Find out what the child likes or wants to do. Go to the movies; that's a *big* treat. My kids love to be hugged. If it's from someone that they're close to, they'll take a hug anytime. Little girls need to be hugged by male friends if they have a comfortable relationship where they can do that. And tell them how pretty they are.
BRANDON:	Support them and understand them. And be a little more patient with them. I think they probably need to be encouraged a little bit more when they do something good. Taking an interest in them, going out of your way to say hi and other little things like that will make them feel accepted.
PATTY:	Take them out to eat or to the movies; be supportive in verbal ways.
MARIAN:	Telling them, "I know you hurt. I'm here to help if I can, and you will make it."
KATHY:	Spending time with them, letting them know that Mom isn't the only adult who loves them. This applies particularly to male friends. I've had people act as though my daughter were more of a bother than anything and that causes real problems. Often I have found myself beginning to treat her badly and to resent her because someone thinks she's too much trouble.

Other Ideas

1. Be generous with smiles, compliments, and expressions of appreciation and approval.

2. Offer to help with homework.

3. Demonstrate your support by attending the child's football game, piano recital, school play, etc.

4. Send cards on special occasions, such as birthdays, Valentine's Day, and Christmas, and notes of encouragement. Phone teens to say "We're thinking about you."

5. Invite the child—with or without an accompanying parent— to come along on family outings or shopping errands or to join your family for dinner and a quiet evening of popcorn and board games. Married couples especially can give teenagers positive examples and hope for their future marriages.

6. If you are at home in the afternoons, welcome the child to spend time at your house after school.

7. Pray for the child and ask the child for personal prayer requests. Check back to see how things are going.

8. Take the child for ice cream or to the movies.

9. Ask for a lesson in something the child does well that you would enjoy knowing more about.

10. Ask the child to pet-sit or plant-sit when you are away. Be sure to pay if you can.

11. Foster any mutual interest you share. Invite the child to work on a project with you.

12. Initiate discussions that encourage the child to talk about personal concerns—interests, friends, and school activities.

13. If you give gifts, consider items that enrich as well as entertain. Ideas: a scholarship to camp, a new Bible, lessons or equipment that will develop a particular talent—ballet shoes, a baseball glove, art supplies, sheet music.

14. Invite the child to spend the weekend with your family. This will give you extended time with the child and be a welcome vacation for the custodial parent.

15. If the parents do not attend church, offer to take the children and introduce them to peers and Sunday school teachers.

16. Words of praise for accomplishments of any sort or for no reason at all can inspire self-confidence.

Kids Helping Kids

Adults can offer children maturity and role models, but unless they experienced divorce as *children,* they can only imagine what the child must be feeling. Sometimes the best person to lean on during a crisis is a friend—a peer—who has experienced the same thing. In addition, because they know what it means to have their homes break up, children of divorce are often highly motivated to reach out to other kids. And it does them good to be able to help someone else.

My panel told me how they would help or have helped other kids and how they have actually received support from others.

SARAH: First of all I would tell them, yes, it's going to be hard and there are going to be nights when you cry yourself to sleep, when you're scared, not knowing what's going to happen next. And I'd tell them, "You know I'm here. If you ever want to talk or just need somebody to listen, to give you some support, I'm here." Every morning in my quiet time I pray for all the kids who are going through the same thing I am because especially if they're non-Christians and they don't have a good church and good support, they're going through just too much that they shouldn't have to go through.

Sarah's desire to help undoubtedly arises from the help she was given by a friend, who "coincidentally" showed up just after Sarah received the news of divorce. Sarah said, "You know, I just couldn't stop crying. And if it hadn't been for my friend Abby, I don't know what I would have done. It must have been God's perfect timing that he allowed her to drive by so I could talk to somebody. We walked around the neighborhood for a while. Basically she just listened. It was just good to have somebody there to listen and give some support."

KIMBERLEE: There's one girl at school whose parents are getting a divorce, and I said, "If you need anybody to talk to, call me. Just whenever, it can be two in the morning. It doesn't matter. Just call me." One time she couldn't cope with it and I said, "I know the feeling." She had to go home from school because it was the day her parents were getting divorced. She was feeling really sick.

PAIGE: I'd tell them that my parents were divorced and how I got through it: Just trust God and he'll work it out somehow.

BRETT: Our youth group went on a retreat a couple weeks ago. I met a girl there from Atlanta, and we've been writing. Her parents are getting a divorce. I don't know if I'm helping her or not. I'm just telling her I understand what she's going through and I'm praying for her.

Judith Wallerstein has noted that once children have experienced divorce they ". . . feel a kinship with all other children of divorce, claiming an identity that sets them apart from their peers."[2] As a result, kids naturally tend to help one another as they interact socially. This unstructured, straight-from-the-heart stuff may be the best medicine of all.

HELPING SINGLE-PARENT FAMILIES

Remember that a child's adjustment to divorce is inseparably intertwined with the mental, physical, emotional, and spiritual well-being of the custodial parent. Anything that aids the parent ultimately benefits the child. Single parents whose emotional needs for friendship and support are met, who have people who can be counted on for practical help, find it easier to meet the needs of their children.

Kathy said, "My close friends have never condemned, and the most helpful things I remember are invitations to dinner, notes in the mail with Scripture verses just to let me know I was loved, small gifts for no reason, and offers to baby-sit so I could have time out. Those meant so much."

Brandon told me, "I get a lot of support from my friends and from people in the church. People encourage me a lot. They say things to me that make me feel like I'm doing something special almost. People say this is really great, here I am taking care of the kids and we seem to be doing okay."

Here are some practical ways to be supportive and helpful. Note that many of them require little time and effort. The main ingredient is genuine concern.

1. Sit with the family in church. Says Sandy, "The first year we sat by ourselves."

2. Introduce them to other single-parent families. They can offer each other mutual support.

3. Call occasionally to see how they are doing. Send cards to let them know you are thinking of them.

4. Offer to baby-sit.

5. If you are at home during the day, volunteer to be on call in case children get sick so the parent does not have to miss work.

6. Take a single parent out for a cup of coffee.

7. Send birthday cards and/or give gifts.

8. If needed, and if possible, help financially at Christmas.

9. Bring dinner and stay and enjoy the fellowship.

10. When the parent is sick, depressed, or overwhelmed with responsibilities, offer to keep the children, run errands, or pitch in.

11. Mothers—let single dads know you're available to answer questions about cooking, laundry, kids, etc.

12. Leave an anonymous gift on the doorstep, perhaps flowers or groceries.

13. Offer your prayers and ask for a list of requests.

14. Buy a book on single parenting and give it as an expression of your support.

15. Give verbal encouragement whenever you see them.

HOW THE CHURCH CAN HELP

Divorce is a spiritual paradox. On one hand, it is a tragedy, tearing apart marriages and families. It causes heartache and suffering for everyone it touches. It keeps us sidetracked: Who can be concerned with the task of reaching the lost when his or her own family is falling apart?

On the other hand—in God's hand—divorce can be a golden opportunity. In the wake of divorce, both adults and children are plowed up in heart, and newly turned "soil" is often receptive to truth. It cries out for something good, something real. Apathetic believers are renewed and the kingdom of heaven is enlarged as those whose hearts were once hard begin asking, seeking, and knocking in an effort to learn if God is real and if he cares for them.

Psalm 119:71 affirms the paradox: "It was good for me to be afflicted so that I might learn your decrees."

Steve's life also affirms the paradox. He said, "I credit my divorce for most if not all of my turnaround in the spiritual area. My kids might not even be going to church now if it weren't for the divorce. I don't condone divorce. I certainly don't recommend it as a way to get spiritual! But I can see that with the way my life was heading and with the friends we had, it would have just continued that way and I may not have turned back to God and to church at all."

Divorce is not just an unfortunate social malady, but also a spiritual battleground where real lives are at stake temporally and eternally. For this reason I would like to suggest two perspectives for any church seeking to help adults and children after divorce.

First, view the task of helping as a redemptive task. Our mandate to function as salt and light in the world goes hand in hand with proclaiming Christ, and in fact opens up many evangelistic opportunities. Beyond salvation, churches can help stimulate spiritual growth, emotional wholeness, and social acceptance—again, a redemptive task, conserving and developing individual potential that might otherwise have been lost to divorce.

Second, never let church membership be a criterion for

receiving help. God places people in our path, and their presence is criterion enough: "Whatever you did for one of the least of these brothers of mine, you did for me" (Matthew 25:40).

HOW ARE WE DOING?

I asked several adults and children to tell me how, or if, their churches had helped them deal with divorce. Here are their comments.

PAUL: age twelve	People at church have really not helped at all.
PAIGE: age ten	They really show that they care. They're nice people.
SANDY: single mom	I got an awful lot of support. My church is super as far as their support of the singles department, and not all churches have that, I know.
ANGELA: age sixteen	They never said anything about it or offered to help in any way.
CAROL: age eighteen	People at church have been helpful at times, but condemning also.
BRENDA: single mom	I've lost faith in what I considered Christian church-going people. Christians have proven to be the least helpful in a crisis such as divorce.
ANNA: age seventeen	People at church know the problems, but no one really understands.
KATHY: single mom	People where I attended during the divorce were so uncomfortable and unfamiliar with how to deal with divorce that they never talked about it, never asked how I was, or if I needed help; it was awful!

So, how are we doing? It seems that the church gets mixed reviews from my "panel of experts." There was nothing mixed about the findings in the Wallerstein study, however: "Although half the families in our study belong to churches or synagogues, not one clergyman came to call on the adults or children during divorce."[3] Clearly, there is room for improvement!

Here are eight things any church can do.

1. *Form an outreach committee.* On behalf of the church, these people would visit single-parent families and families on the verge of divorce. The key to providing genuine help is staying in touch over the long haul. If the committee becomes aware of special needs, it can help direct the family toward the appropriate resources within and outside of the church.

2. *Establish an adopt-a-kid program.* Couples or singles can "adopt" kids from single-parent homes through a matching process based on mutual interests. The adult and child can spend time together pursuing activities they both enjoy. This kind of mentoring relationship, according to Dr. Wallerstein, "is one of the greatest things the church could provide (for) children of divorce."[4]

3. *Give counseling referrals.* Every local church can research the community to provide a list of recommended counselors and therapists. When families need help before, during, and after divorce, the church can make referrals with confidence.

4. *Maintain a list of practical-help resources.* Every church has members with special skills. Discover who is willing to volunteer expertise when pressing needs arise for single-parent families. In a large church, a survey could be taken and the results compiled. When a family needs help with taxes or lawn-mower repair, a phone call can be the link to appropriate help.

5. *Encourage male role models.* By involving more men and couples in children's ministry, we not only provide masculine role models, we also help prevent children from developing a feminized concept of Christianity. Men and couples can be recruited to work in the nursery, teach Sunday school, and lead choirs and clubs.

6. *Establish or expand a church library.* Many books about divorce have been written to help both adults and children. Christian magazines often contain articles helpful to the single parent. A church lending library can be a wonderful resource—

for every family. If your church has a library, add books and magazines that will aid single parents and children of divorce.

7. *Larger churches can offer an adult Sunday school class for singles.* A church that wants to help single-parent families can make a good start by adding a Sunday school class for singles. If there are a lot of singles, add more than one class and divide the groups by age so that members will have more in common. Spouseless people, whether divorced, widowed, or never married, can support each other and socialize together best in a singles' class.

8. *Sensitize children's workers.* A child readily reads the reactions of a Sunday school teacher, choir director, missions club leader, or nursery worker. From interactions with these adults, the child may generalize the supposed reaction of the church as a whole to a parental divorce. If these adults are accepting, loving, and supportive, the child may come to view the church as a source of comfort and encouragement.

Teachers who go the extra mile are most likely to make a lasting positive impression. A child will be grateful for a teacher's kindnesses when facing the crisis of divorce.

Here's how a children's worker might communicate concern to a child:

- Visit the child at home.
- Call or send a postcard after an absence.
- Address the child personally in every class.
- Give a hug—after asking if it would be okay.
- Send a birthday card.
- Establish a positive relationship with the parent. A child may be a single parent's only link to a church; that parent's desire for involvement may depend on how well the child enjoys church activities.
- Demonstrate love no matter how the child behaves.
- Identify your innermost feelings about divorce. Be aware of any attitudes that would hinder your relationship with the child.
- Pray about the child's needs and ask God for wisdom as you seek to touch this young life.

Sarah, fifteen, feels that her personal growth has been

stimulated by the support she's received: "I used to have a very low self-image," she said, "and through the divorce and through a lot of prayer and support from other people, I've finally reached the point where I have a good self-image. I've found a lot of people that are supportive of me; they're my age, too. And maybe that helped. I just know God must really have worked."

May Sarah's words be the report of the children of divorce who cross your path: "I've found a lot of people that are supportive of me. . . . I just know God must really have worked."

APPENDIX

HOW TO KNOW GOD IN A PERSONAL WAY*

Christianity is a personal faith because God is a personal God. God knows everything there is to know about every person alive—including you. He understands your personality, your problems, and your questions. He knows all about your past and your future. He loves you completely. He does not put conditions on his love for you. He loves you whether you have been aware or unaware of him, concerned or unconcerned about him. He loves you no matter what you have done or what you have not done. He just loves you.

God desires to have a meaningful personal relationship with you. He wants to become your closest friend—involved in every aspect of your life. He wants to be someone in whom you can trust and on whom you can rely whether times are good or bad. In short, God wants you to respond to his great love for you: He wants you to know him.

What the Bible Says About Knowing God Personally

Many people react positively to the idea of knowing God in a personal way, but they don't know how to go about establishing a relationship with him. If you are one of these people, there are three things you need to know.

First, you need to understand that there is a barrier between you and God that keeps you from knowing him personally and from experiencing his love. This barrier is the result of the natural human tendency to rebel against God and go one's own way—what the Bible calls sin.

Second, you need to know that there is only one way to remove the sin barrier between you and God. Jesus Christ, God's Son, is himself the only bridge between God and humanity. He willingly died two thousand years ago to remove the barrier of sin between God and the human race. When he died, Christ served as a substitute for you and me. That is, the punishment for our sin fell instead on Jesus.

---

*Adapted from *Have You Heard of the Four Spiritual Laws?* Copyright © Campus Crusade for Christ, 1965.

Third, it is important to realize that Christ's death does not automatically bring about a relationship between a person and God. Each individual is responsible to accept—or reject—Christ's payment for his or her own sins. When one accepts Christ's payment, Christ's death on the cross serves to unite that person in a relationship with God by taking away the sin barrier.

The Bible speaks clearly about God's love for us, about the sin that separates us from him, and about Jesus, through whose death our sins are washed away:

God's love: "For God so loved the world that he gave his one and only Son, that whoever believes in him shall not perish but have eternal life" (John 3:16).

Our sinful nature: "All have sinned and fall short of the glory of God" (Romans 3:23).

The consequences of sin: "The wages of sin is death," being separated from God, both now and in eternity (Romans 6:23).

Jesus, God's provision for our sin: "God demonstrates his own love for us in this: While we were still sinners, Christ died for us" (Romans 5:8).

Jesus, the only way to God: "Jesus answered, 'I am the way and the truth and the life. No one comes to the Father except through me' " (John 14:6).

"Salvation is found in no one else, for there is no other name under heaven given to men by which we must be saved" (Acts 4:12).

Accepting Christ's payment for our sin: Jesus said, "Here I am! I stand at the door and knock. If anyone hears my voice and opens the door, I will come in" (Revelation 3:20).

In this last verse, Jesus makes it clear that he is standing at the door of your life and heart, knocking. He wants to come into your life and forgive your sins, but it is up to you to open the door and receive him as your Savior.

If you welcome Jesus into your heart and life, your sins will be forgiven and the sin barrier between you and God will be removed. John 1:12 says, "To all who received him, to those who believed in his name, he gave the right to become children of God." If you receive Christ, accepting his death as payment for your sins, you'll become part of God's own family. God will be your Father and Friend. As God's child you will have eternal life; you'll be assured of a place in heaven when you die.

How to Receive Christ

All relationships begin with communication. The way we communicate with God is through prayer. Prayer is nothing more than talking to God. God already knows your thoughts and attitudes, so the words you say are not as important as the sincerity of your heart. If you would like to receive Christ as your Savior, you may want to pray the following prayer as an expression of that desire. Or you may want to use your own words.

> Lord Jesus, thank you for your great love for me. I acknowledge that I am a sinner and that my sin has placed a barrier between God and me that only you can take away. I accept your death on the cross as the payment for my own individual sins. I now open the door of my life and ask you to come in. Begin now to make me the kind of person you want me to be. Thank you for giving me eternal life and for making me part of God's own family.

If you sincerely prayed this prayer and invited Jesus Christ to come into your life, he did. You may or may not feel any different. Keep in mind that faith cannot be based on feelings, which waver and change. Instead, Christ and his promises, which never change, are the basis for our faith. Jesus promised to come into your life if you asked him to. He will never leave you, so you never need to invite him in a second time. He is already there and will be with you each day of your life from now on. Welcome to God's family!

What's Next?

There are two more steps you can take now. First, obtain a Bible in a modern translation that you will enjoy reading, such as the *New International Version*. Receiving Christ is the same as being born in a spiritual sense. Spiritual food is found in the Bible. Make a habit of reading a portion of Scripture daily. As you are nourished from the Bible, your relationship with God will grow. In the pages of the Bible God will reveal himself to you in an intimate way.

Second, begin to attend a church that upholds the Bible and teaches people how to receive Christ, as you just did. You may have some negative feelings about church attendance, depending on your past experience, but it's time to approach church involvement with a new outlook. With Christ in your heart, you now have a real reason to worship alongside others who love him. Ask him to guide you in your search for the right church, and don't stop looking until you find one where you feel at home.

NOTES

INTRODUCTION

1. Jane E. Brody, "Children of Divorce: Steps to Help Can Hurt," *New York Times* (23 July 1991): C-1.
2. Andrew J. Cherlin, et al., "Longitudinal Studies of Effects of Divorce on Children in Great Britain and the United States," *Science* (7 June 1991): 1386.
3. *The World Almanac and Book of Facts* (1991), 839–40.
4. Ibid., 840.
5. Diane Crispell, "More Divorces Involve Fewer Children Apiece," *Wall Street Journal* (19 July 1991): B-1.
6. Charlotte A. Schoenborn, "Exposure to Alcoholism in the Family: United States, 1988," *Advance Data*, no. 205, U.S. Department of Health and Human Services, National Center for Health Statistics (30 September 1991).

CHAPTER ONE: THE CHILDREN OF DIVORCE

1. Judith S. Wallerstein and Joan B. Kelly, "California's Children of Divorce," *Psychology Today* (January 1980): 68–69.
2. Marsha Kline, Janet R. Johnston, and Jeanne M. Tschann, "The Long Shadow of Marital Conflict: A Model of Children's Postdivorce Adjustment," *Journal of Marriage and the Family* 53 (May 1991): 297–309.
3. Linda Bird Francke, *Growing Up Divorced* (New York: Linden Press/Simon and Schuster, 1983), 16–17.
4. Judith S. Wallerstein and Joan B. Kelly, *Surviving the Breakup: How Children and Parents Cope with Divorce* (New York: Basic Books, 1980), 36.
5. Ibid., 41–42.
6. Ibid., 42.
7. Ibid.

CHAPTER TWO: A DEATH IN THE FAMILY

1. Bruce Yoder, "My Parents' Divorce Caught Me Off Guard," *Christian Living* (September 1981): 19.
2. Carin Rubenstein, "The Children of Divorce as Adults," *Psychology Today* (January 1980): 75.

3. Judith S. Wallerstein and Sandra Blakeslee, *Second Chances: Men, Women, and Children a Decade After Divorce, Who Wins, Who Loses—And Why* (New York: Ticknor and Fields, 1989), 290.
4. Joseph Bayly, *The Last Thing We Talk About* (Elgin, Ill.: David C. Cook, 1981), 97.
5. Ruth Kopp, *Where Has Grandpa Gone?* (Grand Rapids: Zondervan, 1983), 129.
6. Wallerstein and Blakeslee, *Second Chances*, 13.
7. Barbara Spence, "Death of a Marriage," *HIS* (February 1980): 5.

PART TWO, INTRODUCTION

1. Wallerstein and Blakeslee, *Second Chances*, 15.

CHAPTER THREE: BABIES AND TODDLERS

1. Francke, *Growing Up Divorced, 61–62.*
2. Kay Donahue Jennings, Vaughan Stagg, and Robin E. Connors, "Social Networks and Mothers' Interactions with Their Preschool Children," *Child Development* 62 (1991): 966–78.
3. Ibid., 967.
4. Ross D. Parke and Barbara R. Tinsley, "The Father's Role in Infancy: Determinants of Involvement in Caregiving and Play," in *The Role of the Father in Child Development,* ed. Michael E. Lamb (New York: John Wiley & Sons, 1981), 432, 439, 441.
5. Marie Pichel Warner, M.D., *A Doctor Discusses Breast Feeding* (Chicago: Budlong Press, 1981), 14–16.
6. Frank A. Pederson, "Father Influences Viewed in a Family Context," in Parke and Tinsley, *The Role of the Father,* 310–11.
7. Michael Lewis and Marsha Weinraub, "The Father as a Member of the Child's Social Network," in ibid., 264.
8. Kline, Johnston, and Tschann, "The Long Shadow," 306.
9. Jay Belsky, "Parental and Nonparental Child Care and Children's Socioemotional Development: A Decade in Review," *Journal of Marriage and the Family* 52 (November 1990): 885–903.
10. Kenneth Labick, "Can Your Career Hurt Your Kids?" *Fortune* (May 20, 1991): 40–43.
11. Paul Chance, "Your Child's Self-Esteem," *Parents* (January 1982): 58.
12. Henry B. Biller, *Paternal Deprivation* (Lexington, Mass.: D. C. Heath, 1974), 70.
13. James Dobson, *Dr. Dobson Answers Your Questions* (Wheaton, Ill.: Tyndale House, 1982), 76.
14. Wallerstein and Blakeslee, *Second Chances,* 175.

CHAPTER FOUR: PRESCHOOLERS (TWO- TO FOUR-YEAR-OLDS)

1. Wallerstein and Blakeslee, *Second Chances,* 175.
2. Wallerstein and Kelly, *Surviving the Breakup,* 39.
3. Cathy Carter, "Children Often Are Among the Victims of Divorce," *Winston-Salem Journal* (11 October 1981): E-1.
4. Henry B. Biller, *Father, Child, and Sex Role: Paternal Determinants of Personality Development* (Lexington, Mass.: D. C. Heath, 1971), 6.
5. Wallerstein and Kelly, *Surviving the Breakup,* 61.
6. Ibid., 101.

CHAPTER FIVE: (FIVE- TO EIGHT-YEAR-OLDS)

1. Wallerstein and Kelly, *Surviving the Breakup,* 65–66.
2. Francke, *Growing Up Divorced,* 51–52.
3. Wallerstein and Kelly, *Surviving the Breakup,* 71.
4. "Divorce: Kids in the Middle," Showtime (March 26, 1983).
5. Francke, *Growing Up Divorced,* 102.

CHAPTER SIX: PRETEENS (NINE- TO TWELVE-YEAR-OLDS)

1. Brody, "Children of Divorce: Steps to Help Can Hurt," C-1.
2. Wallerstein and Kelly, *Surviving the Breakup,* 51–52.
3. Francke, *Growing Up Divorced,* 119.
4. Linda Asmussen and Reed Larson, "The Quality of Family Time Among Young Adolescents in Single-Parent and Married-Parent Families," *Journal of Marriage and the Family* 53 (November 1991): 1021–30.
5. Ross Campbell, Parenting Seminar, Calvary Baptist Church, Winston-Salem, N.C. (21–22 November 1981).
6. Wallerstein and Blakeslee, *Second Chances,* 163.

CHAPTER SEVEN: TEENAGERS

1. Yoder, "My Parents' Divorce Caught Me Off Guard," 1 8.
2. Wallerstein and Kelly, *Surviving the Breakup,* 82.
3. Wallerstein and Blakeslee, *Second Chances,* 100.
4. Ibid., 169.
5. Ibid., 84.
6. William J. Doherty and Richard H. Needle, "Psychological Adjustment and Substance Use Among Adolescents Before and After a Parental Divorce," *Child Development* 62 (1991): 328–37.
7. Leslie Williams, *Which Way Is Home?* (Nashville: Thomas Nelson, 1981), 61–64.

8. Wallerstein and Kelly, *Surviving the Breakup,* 91.
9. Doherty and Needle, "Psychological Adjustment," 335.
10. Wallerstein and Blakeslee, *Second Chances,* 56–64.
11. Brody, "Children of Divorce: Steps to Help Can Hurt," C-9.
12. Barbara Kantrowitz, et al., "Breaking the Divorce Cycle," *Newsweek* (January 9, 1992): 49–50.
13. Barbara Kantrowitz, "Children of the Aftershock: Exploring the Long-Term Effects of Divorce," *Newsweek* (7 February 1989): 61.

CHAPTER EIGHT: REPORT CARD BLUES

1. Wallerstein and Kelly, *Surviving the Breakup,* 267–68.
2. Dobson, *Dr. Dobson Answers Your Questions,* 186.
3. Larry Kortering, Norris Haring, and Alan Klockars, "The Identification of High School Dropouts Identified as Learning Disabled: Evaluating the Utility of a Discriminant Analysis Function," *Exceptional Children* 58, no. 5 (March/April 1992): 425.
4. "Divorce: At What Cost?" sidebar in *Focus on the Family* (April 1992): 11.
5. Biller, *Paternal Deprivation,* 88.
6. Ibid., 121.
7. Ibid., 137.
8. Ibid., 130.

CHAPTER NINE: WHERE IS GOD?

1. Francke, *Growing Up Divorced,* 16.
2. Gary D. Chapman, *Hope for the Separated* (Chicago: Moody Press, 1982), 56–57.
3. Debbie Barr, "Hope for the Separated: An Interview with Dr. Gary D. Chapman," *Family Life Today* (February 1982): 25.
4. Dobson, *Dr. Dobson Answers Your Questions,* 43.
5. Tim LaHaye, *Understanding the Male Temperament* (Old Tappan, N.J.: Fleming H. Revell, 1977), 19.
6. Roger Rosenblatt, "Children of War," *Time* (11 January 1982): 36–37, 39, 50.
7. Bruce Yoder, "When Divorce Drives Its Wedge," *With* (May 1983): 14.

CHAPTER TEN: MONEY MATTERS

1. Wallerstein and Kelly, *Surviving the Breakup,* 172.
2. Richard H. Stewart, "Many Discover Divorce Means Economic Woe," *Winston-Salem Journal* (10 February 1983): 10.

3. Laura Ellen Harris, "House Committee Debates U.S. Family Norms," *Population Today* (April 1992): 5.

4. Jay D. Teachman, "Who Pays? Receipt of Child Support in the United States," *Journal of Marriage and the Family* (August 1991): 759.

5. David H. Demo, "Parent-Child Relations: Assessing the Recent Changes," *Journal of Marriage and the Family* 54 (February 1992): 104–17.

6. "Second Thoughts on Divorce," *The Economist* (17 August 1991): A-23.

7. "Divorce: At What Cost?" sidebar in *Focus on the Family* (April 1992): 11.

8. Biller, "Father Absence, Divorce, and Personality Development," 531.

9. Wallerstein and Kelly, *Surviving the Breakup,* 230–31.

10. Henry B. Biller and Dennis Meredith, *Father Power* (New York: David McKay, 1974), 139–40.

11. Wallerstein and Kelly, *Surviving the Breakup,* 124.

12. Biller and Meredith, *Father Power,* 140.

13. Jay D. Teachman, "Contributions to Children by Divorced Fathers," *Social Problems* 38, no. 3 (August 1991): 361.

14. Ibid., 369.

CHAPTER ELEVEN: THE GRANDPARENT CONNECTION

1. Wallerstein and Blakeslee, *Second Chances,* 111.

2. Archibald D. Hart, *Children and Divorce* (Waco: Word Books, 1982), 21.

3. *The World Almanac and Book of Facts,* 1991, 842.

4. Karen Youngblood, "Child Custody: Placements with Grandparents Rise," *Winston-Salem Journal* (3 September 1991): A-1.

5. Leola Archer, "Something Special," *Family Life Today* (November 1982): 24.

CHAPTER TWELVE: SOLO PARENTING

1. Francke, *Growing Up Divorced,* 250.

2. Hetherington, Cox, and Cox, "The Aftermath of Divorce," *mother/child father/child Relationships,* ed. Joseph H. Stevens, Jr., and Marilyn Matthews (Washington: National Association for the Education of Young Children, 1978), 170.

3. Kline, Johnston, and Tschann, "The Long Shadow," 297–309.

4. Brody, "Children of Divorce: Steps to Help Can Hurt," C-9.

5. Wallerstein and Blakeslee, *Second Chances,* 238.

6. Chapman, *Hope for the Separated,* 101–2.

7. Wallerstein and Blakeslee, *Second Chances,* 302.

8. James C. Young and Muriel E. Hamilton, "Paternal Behavior: Implications for Childrearing Practice," *mother/child father/child Relationships,* 141.

9. Dick Thompson, "In California: Unswinging Singles," *Time* (15 June 1981): 8.

10. Stephanie Simon, "Joint Custody Loses Favor for Increasing Children's Feelings of Being Torn Apart," *Wall Street Journal* (15 July 1991): B-1.

11. Christy M. Buchanan, Eleanor E. Maccoby, and Sanford M. Dornbusch, "Caught Between Parents: Adolescents' Experience in Divorced Homes," *Child Development* 62 (1991): 1008–29.

CHAPTER THIRTEEN: PRESCRIPTION FOR PARENTS

1. "The Children of Divorce," *Business Week* (2 April 1979): 103.
2. Wallerstein and Blakeslee, *Second Chances,* 285.
3. Ibid., 285–87.
4. Jo Woestendiek, "What About the Kids?: The Effects of Divorce Are Lasting, *Winston-Salem Journal* (7 April 1991): G-1.
5. Wallerstein and Blakeslee, *Second Chances,* 305.
6. Hart, *Children and Divorce,* 38.

CHAPTER FOURTEEN: FAMILY HEIRLOOMS

1. Nell Perry Barbee, "Youngsters Respond to 'How Did Divorce Affect You?' " *Winston-Salem Journal* (4 April 1983): 18.
2. Rubenstein, "The Children of Divorce as Adults," 74.
3. Ibid., 75.
4. Cathy Carter, "In the Aftermath, Stress and Strain Face the Family," *Winston-Salem Journal* (11 October 1981): E-1.
5. Deidre S. Laiken, "Daughters of Divorce," *Glamour* (November 1981): 286.
6. Young and Hamilton, *Paternal Behavior,* 142.
7. James D. Mallory, Jr., with James C. Hefley, *Untwisted Living* (Wheaton, Ill.: Victor Books, 1982), 131.
8. Biller, *Paternal Deprivation,* 115.
9. Francke, *Growing Up Divorced,* 26.
10. Barbara Kantrowitz, et al., "Breaking the Divorce Cycle," 49–50.
11. Kenneth S. Wuest, "Bypaths in the Greek New Testament," *Wuest's Word Studies in the Greek New Testament,* vol. 3 (Grand Rapids: Eerdmans, 1973), 73.

CHAPTER FIFTEEN: A POUND OF CURE: HOW TEACHERS, FRIENDS, AND CHURCHES CAN HELP

1. Paul R. Amato, "The 'Child of Divorce' as Person Prototype: Bias in the Recall of Information about Children in Divorced Families," *Journal of Marriage and the Family* 53 (February 1991): 59–69.
2. Wallerstein and Blakeslee, *Second Chances,* 23.
3. Ibid., 7.
4. Jim Smoke, "Suggestions for an Effective Ministry with Children of Divorce," *Single Adult Ministries Journal* (March 1990): 4.

MATT AND KIM

A READ-ALOUD STORY
FOR CHILDREN

This story is designed to be read aloud to preschool or early school-age children, preferably with separate sittings for each chapter. The discussion questions can be used as teaching aids and to help you discover how a child is feeling. The text is approximately third- to fourth-grade reading level. Children in these grades may want to read it for themselves.

1

Bad News!

Bam! The screen door slammed behind Matt as he ran into the kitchen.

"Mommy," he called, "can I go play with Jeff?"

Mom was coming up the stairs from the basement. She was carrying a basket of laundry. When she got to the top of the stairs, she set the basket on the floor. Then she sat down on a kitchen chair.

"Matt," she said, "come here a minute."

Matt walked over to where Mommy was sitting. She put her arm around his waist. In a soft voice she said, "Your daddy and I have something important to tell you and Kim. Would you ask Kim to come inside?"

"Sure, Mommy," said Matt. He headed toward the door, wondering what Mommy and Daddy wanted to talk about. Maybe it was about the camping trip they had planned!

No, Matt thought to himself. *That can't be it. Mommy seemed sort of sad. If it were about the camping trip, she would be happy.*

Suddenly Matt felt worried. He tried to remember if he and

Kim had done something wrong. Matt stepped outside. His sister, Kim, was playing in the sandbox.

Matt called, "Kim, Mommy says to come inside. They want to talk to us."

"Okay," said Kim. She jumped up and brushed the sand off her jeans.

Soon Matt and Kim joined Mommy and Daddy in the living room. King, the family dog, was lying on the floor near Daddy's feet. His tail began to thump on the floor as Matt reached down to scratch his ears.

Except for the thump of King's tail, the room was quiet. Daddy took a deep breath. Then he put one arm around Kim and one arm around Matt.

"Your mother and I love you both very much," he began. "And we will *always* love you. Nothing can change that. You make us very happy. We always thank God that he gave us two very special children."

Matt grinned at Kim. They both knew how much Mommy and Daddy loved them. It made them feel all warm and good inside whenever they said something like that.

Their dad continued, "Now, I have to tell you something important. It will be very hard to say, so listen carefully." He had a serious look on his face. Matt looked at Mommy. She had a serious look on her face, too.

Daddy continued, "Your mother and I have had many problems being married to each other. We have tried very hard to work these problems out for a long time. These are *grown-up* problems. They have nothing to do with you children. The problems are only between your mom and me.

"We wish we could solve these problems, but we can't. So we have made a big decision. This decision will affect all of us— Mommy, Daddy, Matt, and Kim. We feel that the only solution to our problems is for your mom and me to get a divorce."

Kim and Matt could not believe their ears! Had Daddy said "divorce"? For a minute nobody said a word. Matt wanted to shout, "No, no! You can't," but the words got stuck in his throat. Kim wanted to run up to her room and hug her teddy bear, but she could not move. Her eyes filled with tears.

Mommy squeezed Kim's hand and gave her a tissue. Mom

said, "Next Saturday your father will be moving into an apartment. It's not far away, just four blocks. You can walk over to see him any time you want. You children and King will live here with me."

When Matt found his voice again, he asked, "But *why?* Why can't we all live together? Why do you have to get a divorce?"

"Sometimes parents can't work out their problems, Matt," said Daddy. "Sometimes they try very hard, but they fail. That's what happened to us."

Agreeing, Mommy said, "We're sorry it has to be this way. We know this is sad news for you. We know you feel very upset. Your father and I feel bad and upset, too. But we still think getting a divorce is what we should do. We are unhappy being married to each other. We think it will be better if we live apart."

Kim asked, "Do you still love us? Will you still be our mommy and daddy?"

"Oh yes!" said Mommy and Daddy at the same time.

"We'll always love you," said Daddy. "We will always be your mom and dad. We'll always take good care of you."

Mommy added, "Divorce can change many things, but it can never change our love for you!"

QUESTIONS

1. What was the bad news that Matt and Kim got?
2. Did you ever get bad news like this?
3. When Matt heard about the divorce, he was so surprised that he couldn't talk. Kim wanted to run away, but instead she started to cry. When you found out that your parents were going to get a divorce, what did you do?
4. What did the parents in this story say that divorce could never change?
5. Do you think the divorce in your family changed anything? What do you think it changed?

2

Is It My Fault?

Matt opened his sleepy eyes. The sunshine coming through the window in his room told him that it was morning.

Today is Saturday, he thought happily. *Kim and I can watch cartoons on TV!* Then he remembered, *Today is the day Daddy moves into his apartment.*

Suddenly Matt felt very sad. He hugged his pillow tightly. Soon the pillowcase was wet with tears. Matt tried hard to think of something he could do to make his daddy change his mind about the divorce. He thought for a long time. Then he got an idea.

Matt jumped out of bed and dressed in a hurry. He ran across the hall to Kim's room.

Matt knocked on her door. There was no answer. He opened the door just a crack. Kim was not in her room.

Oh well, Matt thought. *No time to waste. I'll just have to do it by myself.*

Matt went to the closet where Mommy kept the soaps and broom. He took out a bucket, a scrub brush, and some soap. He carried them outside and set them in the grass. He filled the bucket with water from the garden hose. Then he poured in lots of soap and swished up lots of suds.

Matt picked up the bucket—heavy and hard to carry. Water sloshed over the sides until his jeans and sneakers were soaked. Oh so carefully, he walked to the garage. He set the bucket down and took a rest.

Matt looked at the side of the garage. It was covered with splashes of paint. Blue. White. Yellow. The paint hadn't been there long, only a few weeks. Matt had tried to paint a beautiful picture on the garage wall. He wanted it to look like the picture on the wall of the bank downtown. It was called a mural. But when he finished painting, it didn't look like a mural at all. It was a terrible mess! And when his dad saw it, he had been very angry. He had scolded Matt and spanked him. Matt had never seen his daddy so angry!

Now Matt thought, *If I can just get this paint off of the garage, then Daddy won't have anything to be mad about. Then he won't want to move into an apartment. And Mommy and Daddy won't get a divorce!*

Matt worked hard. He scrubbed and scrubbed. But the paint wasn't coming off!

Just then, Matt heard a noise. He turned around, but he didn't see anything. He started to scrub again. Then he heard the sound again. He put the scrub brush down and listened hard. There it was again. It sounded like Kim's voice. But where was she?

"Kim, is that you?" he called in a loud whisper.

"Yes. I'm up here."

Matt looked up into the big tree next to the garage. Kim was in the tree house Dad had built for them. When she saw Matt, she climbed down.

She said, "Matt, I know why Mommy and Daddy are getting a divorce! It's because of me. I'm always losing my toys, and my room is messy. And I don't always come right away when they call me. And I wouldn't go to bed when the baby-sitter was here. I was up in the tree house praying that God would forgive me for being so bad. And for causing the divorce." Kim started to cry.

"No, Kim," said Matt. "The divorce is not your fault—it's

mine! They're getting a divorce because I painted on the garage and made Daddy mad. And now the paint won't come off!" Then Matt began to cry, too.

Just then Daddy came out of the house, carrying a box to the car. He saw Matt and Kim crying and came over to them.

"Let's sit down under the tree," he said. So Matt and Kim and Daddy all sat down. They leaned on the trunk of the big, old tree by the garage.

"Tell me why you are crying," said Daddy.

"I know the divorce is my fault, Daddy!" said Matt. "But I'm trying to clean the paint off the garage."

"The divorce is *my* fault!" said Kim. "But I promise that I won't lose any more toys, and I'll keep my room clean. I'll even come right away when you call me. And I'll be good when the baby-sitter comes."

Daddy looked at Matt. Then he looked at Kim. "You are both wrong," he said. "The divorce is not Matt's fault *or* Kim's fault. It has nothing to do with the paint on the garage or losing toys. In fact, it has nothing to do with anything either of you has *ever* done. Don't think that Mommy and I are getting a divorce because of you or because of something you did. It's not true."

"I know divorce is hard for you to understand," said Daddy. "But you should always remember this: There is nothing children can do to cause a divorce to happen. Divorce is not your fault."

QUESTIONS

1. Why did Matt think Mommy and Daddy were getting a divorce?
2. Why did Kim think Mommy and Daddy were getting a divorce?
3. Who was right?
4. Have you ever thought that the divorce in your family was your fault?
5. Read the last two sentences in the story again. What did Matt and Kim's Daddy tell them? Is he right?

3
Why Do I Feel So Bad?

On a hot summer day Matt and Kim went to the pool in the park with their friends Jeff and Maria. Jeff was diving off the side of the pool. Maria was standing in line to go down the sliding board. But Matt and Kim were just lying in the sun. They didn't feel like having fun. They were thinking about the divorce.

Matt liked to swim. But today swimming seemed boring. He opened a comic book and started to read. He liked to read comic books when he was lying by the pool. But today comic books seemed boring, too. He gave them to Kim.

"Want to read these?" he asked.

"No, thanks," said Kim. "I don't feel like it either."

Suddenly Kim jumped up. Feeling really mean, she ran over to the side of the pool and pushed Maria in!

"What's the big idea?" shouted Maria as she climbed out of the pool. Kim ran away but Maria chased her. To get back at her, Maria wanted to push Kim in the pool.

Both girls knew that running was not allowed. It even said NO RUNNING in big letters right on the cement by the pool. Kim read the words as she ran across them. Right then she didn't care whether she obeyed or not. She just felt mean and unhappy inside.

Suddenly a younger girl walked out in front of Kim and Maria. Maria saw her and stopped running. But Kim didn't see her. Before anyone could say "stop," Kim ran right into the girl and knocked her down.

The lifeguard blew a whistle and came running. The girl's mother came running. Maria and Jeff and Matt came running, too. Everyone could see that the girl had skinned her knees. There was even blood on the cement.

Suddenly Kim didn't feel so mean anymore. Instead, she felt very sorry. She said she was sorry, but it didn't seem to help much. She offered to go inside with the mother to wash the girl's knees, but the mother said no.

The lifeguard marched Kim and Maria to the lifeguard chair. "You have broken the rules. That means you cannot come back to the pool for the rest of the week. That goes for both of you."

Maria got mad.

"But it's not my fault!" shouted Maria. "Kim was the one who pushed me in the pool. And she was the one who ran into the kid!"

"Sorry," said the lifeguard. "Rules are rules."

Kim felt very bad about pushing Maria, getting her into trouble, and making her mad. She was afraid she'd lost a friend. She felt sorry for hurting the little girl. She wished she had stayed at home instead of coming to the pool.

Kim and Maria went to pick up their towels. They told Jeff and Matt that they had to leave. The boys said they would leave, too. They called Maria's mom to take them home.

In the car, Kim said, "Maria, I'm awfully sorry."

Maria didn't say anything, and Kim felt worse. But finally Maria said, "That's okay. Just don't ever push me in the water again!"

"I won't," Kim promised.

When Kim got home, she told Mommy what had happened.

"Kim, what got into you?" asked Mommy.

"I don't know," said Kim sadly. "I just know I feel bad

and mean inside since Daddy left. Sometimes I don't understand why I do the things I do. I don't feel happy."

Matt had been listening. "I don't feel happy either, Mommy," he said. "Nothing seems fun anymore. I don't even feel like playing with King."

"Why do we feel so bad, Mommy?" asked Kim and Matt.

Mommy thought about the question. "When there is a divorce, everyone in the family feels bad," she said. "But not everyone feels bad in the same way. Some people want to be alone instead of being with their friends. Things that used to be fun for them might seem boring. Is that how you feel, Matt?"

"Yeah," he answered.

"Other people feel angry inside. The anger makes them say or do things they wouldn't normally do. Sound like you, Kim?"

"Yes, Mom."

"The feelings a family gets after a divorce are the same kinds of feelings you might get when someone dies. The sad-mad feelings are called grief. They come because you miss having Daddy here every day. And you miss the way our family used to be. Sometimes feelings of grief take a long time to go away."

"You have grief feelings too, Mommy?" asked Matt.

"Yes, I do," said Mommy. "Some days I feel very sad. Then angry. Then other days I feel happier."

Kim said, "Some days I feel scared. I don't know what will happen next."

Matt said, "Some days I feel lonely, especially if Daddy doesn't call us."

"I'm glad we can talk about our feelings," said Kim. "It makes me feel better."

"Me, too," said Matt.

"Me, too," said Mommy.

"Woof!" said King.

QUESTIONS

1. Who felt bad in this story?
2. Why did they feel bad?

3. Matt and Kim felt many things after their parents got divorced: sad, angry, mean, lonely, bored. What feelings do you have?

4. When we have bad feelings we sometimes say or do things we later wish we hadn't said or done. What did Kim do that she wished she hadn't done?

5. Bad feelings sometimes keep us from enjoying things we usually enjoy. What did Matt's bad feelings keep him from enjoying?

6. Was Kim right or wrong when she pushed Maria into the pool? Can we help it when we get bad feelings? Do we have to *act* on our bad feelings? What could Kim have done instead?*

7. Matt and Kim felt better when they talked about their bad feelings. Do you feel better when you talk about your bad feelings?

---

*This question can be used to help children see that in spite of their feelings they are still responsible for their actions.

4
Will Mommy and Daddy Get Back Together?

It was a rainy day. Mommy said that Kim and Matt had to stay inside and play.

"What can we play?" asked Matt.

"I know," said Kim. "Let's color in our new coloring books."

Matt went to get the crayons. Kim went to get the coloring books. Then they lay on the living room floor and began to color.

Kim colored a picture of puppies and kittens. Matt colored a picture of a family having fun on a picnic. The family had a mother, a father, a boy, and a girl. They reminded Matt of Mommy, his dad, Kim, and himself. The dog in the picture even looked like King.

Matt colored the mother's hair light brown, just like Mommy's. He colored the father's hair dark brown, just like his dad's. And he colored the boy's hair and the girl's hair yellow because he and Kim had blond hair. He made the dog white with a black spot on his tail, like King. Matt worked hard on his picture. When he got done he showed it to Kim.

"Matt, it looks like our family!" she cried.

"I know," said Matt. "But our family isn't all together anymore like this one is." Matt's voice sounded sad.

For a moment, Kim felt sad, too. Then she had a very happy thought. "Maybe Mommy and Daddy will get back together!" she said.

Matt liked that idea. "Yeah! Maybe they will." Now Matt's voice sounded excited. "Maybe Daddy will come back home, and we can all be together again."

Kim was getting excited, too. She said, "Remember the day I pushed Maria in the pool? For a while she was mad at me. But then we made up. Maybe Mommy and Daddy will make up, too!"

Kim and Matt wanted Mommy and Daddy to get back together more than anything in the whole world. They wanted their daddy to come home. They wanted their family to be the way it was before the divorce.

Matt said, "When I blow out the candles on my next birthday cake, I am going to make a very special wish. I am going to wish for Daddy to come home."

"Me, too," said Kim. "Then maybe Mommy and Daddy will get back together very soon."

When the rain stopped, Mommy said that the children could go outside to play.

"Let's go next door and see Mrs. Green," said Matt. Kim agreed. They liked Mrs. Green, their special friend.

Mrs. Green was out, sitting on her porch. Matt and Kim walked over and sat at her feet.

"What have you two been up to on such a rainy day?" asked Mrs. Green.

The children told her about their new coloring books. They told her about Matt's picture that looked like their family. And they told her that they were going to wish very hard for Mommy and Daddy to get back together soon.

"Well," said Mrs. Green, "that would be very nice. But a divorce is a divorce."

Matt and Kim were puzzled. "What do you mean?" they asked.

Mrs. Green explained, "When a husband and a wife get

divorced, it means they are not married anymore. A divorce means that the marriage is over."

Matt and Kim did not like what Mrs. Green said.

"When Maria and I were mad at each other, we made up," said Kim. "We're still friends. Why couldn't Mommy and Daddy make up, too?"

"Divorce is different," said Mrs. Green. "Divorce is more than an argument. Divorce means that a marriage has come to an end. You could even say that the marriage has died. Sometimes a mommy and a daddy can be friends after a divorce. But they are not married anymore—and they never will be."

"Oh," said Matt.

"Oh," said Kim.

Mrs. Green gave the children a hug. "I know you feel disappointed," she said. "I know you wish that your family could be together the way it was before. That wish won't come true. But here's a happy thought. Now you have two homes: one with your daddy and one with your mommy. That makes your family very, very special."

Kim and Matt smiled. Mrs. Green was right. Their family *was* very, very special.

QUESTIONS

1. What did Kim and Matt wish Mommy and Daddy would do?
2. Do you ever wish your mommy and daddy would get back together?
3. When a husband and a wife get divorced, are they still married?
4. How is divorce different from an argument?
5. What did Mrs. Green tell Matt and Kim when they told her their wish that Mommy and Daddy would get back together?
6. Kim and Matt think their family is very special. What makes your family special?